Bo and Judson have put together an awesome resource that is both relevant and biblical. If youth leaders are going to break through to this generation, they must break from purely program-driven paradigms and move to an incarnational model of discipleship. *The Be-With Factor* takes you back to one of the foundational principles of Jesus' ministry: life on life for life. This book will inspire, equip, and transform you.

Greg Stier, Founder and President,
Dare2Share Ministries

"Being-with" is a fundamental element for building an effective relational ministry. *The Be-With Factor* practically illustrates for youth workers how to implement this critical aspect into ministry through helpful examples and tools, especially as one pursues mentoring relationships.

Lynn Ziegenfuss, Director of Mentoring,
National Network of Youth Ministries

Say the word "mentor" and people are often intimidated. But ask a Christian adult to "Be-With" a few students and simply invite them into their everyday life, and the job seems doable. Thanks to Bo and Judson, you now have a complete guide for this relational journey. Use this book to help you make an eternal impact on the lives of young students.

Doug Fields, Pastor to Students, Saddleback Church;
President, Simply Youth Ministry

Bo Boshers epitomizes empowering individuals to prepare for the future by helping answer their most intimate and fundamental questions. *The Be-With Factor* and *The Be-With Factor Student Guide* provide biblical insights with superglue. This will stick with you through all the ages.

Dr. Jay Strack, Founder and President,
Studentleadership.net

If we are going to raise up a new generation of Christ-centered leaders, it isn't going to happen by having bigger and better youth ministry programs. Leaders spending time mentoring a small group of students will develop the leaders of today and tomorrow. Bo and Judson do a great job helping youth leaders get back to the basics of Jesus' model—pouring into a small group of students and giving you a resource to help make a difference for eternity.

Andy Stephenson, PhD, North American Leader
of Youth and Family Ministry, Church
of God Ministries, Anderson, IN

It's one thing to write about mentoring; it's another thing to model and live it as a lifestyle. Bo Boshers is the right person to listen to and be trained by in becoming an effective mentor to students in this generation. *The Be-With Factor* is a must-read.

Josh McDowell, author and speaker

One of the most disturbing truths of my twenty years in national and urban youth ministry is the sad reality of the great numbers of students who fall away from the faith after completing high school. No clearer picture could be painted on how to authentically love our students than the tested precepts unfolded in this book. *The Be-With Factor* cleverly answers the how, what, where, and why of discipleship/mentorship. No more guesswork or room for intimidation after diving into the insights of *The Be-With Factor*. This volume is a must-read for my team as we endeavor to reach the fatherless for the Father. Undoubtedly *The Be-With Factor* should find a home in the library of any youth worker serious about kingdom business.

Steve Fitzhugh, President, The House,
Washington, DC

Students regard your very presence in their lives as a sign of caring and connectedness. The greatest impact in anyone's life is almost always from a significant person who took time to "be-with" them. Bo and Judson not only have written a most excellent book on mentoring, they live it.

Jim Burns, PhD, President, HomeWord

In a world where so many people feel "father-less" Bo Boshers has given us a pile of insights about how to get close, how to build, how to point the younger generation to Christ and ultimate usefulness in the kingdom. *The Be-With Factor* needs to be on the required reading list of every man or woman called to student ministries.

Gordon MacDonald, author and speaker

thebe✕withfactor

Also by Bo Boshers:

Student Ministry for the 21st Century
(with Kim Anderson)

Doing Life with God, Volumes 1 and 2
(with Kim Anderson)

Becoming a Contagious Christian Youth Edition
(with Mark Mittelberg, Lee Strobel, and Bill Hybels)

Vision Moments
(with Keith Cote)

*G-Force: Taking Your Relationship with God
to a New Level*

Also by Judson Poling:

Walking with God series
(with Don Cousins)

Tough Questions series
(with Garry Poole)

Pursuing Spiritual Transformation series
(with John Ortberg and Laurie Pederson)

Interpretation: Discovering the Bible for Yourself
(from the Bible 101 series)

*Taking the Old Testament Challenge:
A Daily Reading Guide*
(with John Ortberg)

The Journey: A Bible for the Spiritually Curious
(general editor)

thebe✕withfactor

mentoring students in everyday life

bo boshers & judson poling

ZONDERVAN™

GRAND RAPIDS, MICHIGAN 49530 USA

WILLOW
Willow Creek Resources

ZONDERVAN.COM/
AUTHORTRACKER

ZONDERVAN™

The Be-With Factor
Copyright © 2006 by Willow Creek Association

Requests for information should be addressed to:
Zondervan, *Grand Rapids, Michigan 49530*

Library of Congress Cataloging-in-Publication Data

Boshers, Bo.
    The be-with factor: mentoring students in everyday life / Bo Boshers and Judson
Poling.—1st ed.
      p. cm.
    ISBN-13: 978-0-310-27160-4
    ISBN-10: 0-310-27160-6
    1. Church work with teenagers. 2. Church work with students. 3. Mentoring in church
work. I. Poling, Judson. II. Title.
    BV4447.B682 2006
    259'.23—dc22
                            2005030107

Interior design by Mark Sheeres

Printed in the United States of America

07 08 09 10 11 • 10 9 8 7 6 5 4

A thank you to ...

Bo

To Dan Webster, a true example of a mentor and authentic Christ-follower. Thank you for investing in my life, my friend. I will forever be indebted to you.

Judson

To Barry Zuercher, who explained the gospel in a way that was clear, with a heart that was kind, and who led me in the early years. We've lost touch, but I've never forgotten.

To our families ...

Bo

Thank you Brandon, Tiffany, and Trevor for your total support and encouragement. I love you and am so proud to be your dad. And to my wife and best friend, Gloria —you are an amazing woman. Thank you for always being there for me—I love you.

Judson

Anna and Ryan, one more time: "There's nothing you could e-v-e-r do to make me stop loving you." Deb, every day since you said "Yes" overlooking the lights of Chattanooga, I've wondered how I could love you more; but then every day, I find out.

table of contents

introduction
what does it take to be a mentor?

The fact that you're reading this book says you care about today's generation of students. Whether you work full-time or part-time as a youth pastor, volunteer with the ministry, have a student living with you, or are a parent of a teen, the purpose of this book is to help you accomplish the goal of becoming a difference-maker to this generation. There are many good programs and strategies in youth ministries, but we believe there's no better way to accomplish spiritual transformation in the life of a student than through the Be-With Factor.

The apostle Paul wrote, "Whatever you have learned or received or heard from me, or seen in me — put into practice" (Phil. 4:9). For all of us who serve in some capacity in youth ministry, we've got a tough question to consider: *How can students put into practice what they have not seen up close?* If Paul's example in this verse is to be followed in our day, the solution seems obvious. Someone needs to get up close to students so they know what they need to put into practice. We believe this person is you. Whatever your current role with students, we want to see you get in the game of life-transformation through mentoring.

Most people taking an honest look at the state of youth ministry today admit there's a problem. If what we want to accomplish is deep life-change and spiritual maturity, we are not winning the battle. More and better programs are not the answer. We believe that mentoring may just be the spark to set ablaze the needed fire of revival. The Be-With Factor is our best and brightest light in a dark world of students drifting farther and farther from God.

And what is the Be-With Factor? It is simply the act of "being-with" a few students and modeling for them how a Christ-follower thinks and acts. It's taking a student or two along with you in some of your routine activities, connecting with them personally as you go through your day. Jesus chose men and women to *be with* him. We're asking you to do what Jesus did ... and that's to "be-with" a few so lasting life-change happens.

We pray that you would become a mentor—that you would model for this up-and-coming generation what being a Christ-follower is all about. We also hope you'll give a copy of this book to others and encourage them to do the same—to step onto the playing field and make a difference one life at a time.

We are not content just to motivate and inspire you. We want to give you practical tools. This book has clear guidelines so that the mentoring relationship starts well, stays safe, and makes a difference. This book contains a step-by-step plan for identifying the student you need to invest in and understanding what it takes to "be-with" them in order to create life-changing moments together.

We also included a six-lesson meeting plan to start you off, with six separate Be-With scenarios. These outlines are found in the appendix and can be used with the companion book *The Be-With Factor Student Guide: Six Questions Students Need to Ask About Life with God* to give you everything you need to begin a mentoring relationship.

Once you've read this book, our prayer again is that you would allow 2 Timothy 2:2 to guide your life: "The things you have heard me say in the presence of many witnesses entrust to reliable men who will also be qualified to teach others." The ministry of entrusting spiritual life and treasure to a few others is an honor, and it is God's way of building into the next generation. We realize that if you choose to do this, you will face uncertainties and obstacles. We've tried to anticipate those difficulties and address them in our book. We're convinced that with a little coaching —and with your caring heart and willing spirit—you can do this.

We are not calling exceptional people to do the impossible. We are inviting ordinary people to make an extraordinary difference by copying the way of Jesus ... and that is to "be-with" a few.

One more thing. We asked mentors from around the country to send us stories of how their investment in a few lives made a difference. Their stories are scattered throughout the book. We received more anecdotes than we could use, but every story was a reminder of mentoring's potency and power, and we are grateful. You men and women let us see into your lives—both you and those you mentored—and now many more will catch the vision and share the blessing of what can happen in intentional mentoring relationships. Thanks to: Trevor Murphy, John Wooden, Coleman Falco, Wayne Bushnell, Alex Puatu, Dave O'Vell,

Aaron Winkle, Dave Keehn, Tim Homa, Mike Berry, Chris Tomp-kins, Kevin Carter, Deb Matterom, Paul Jansen Van Rensburg, Sibyl Towner, Ronnie Rothe, Ann Healing, Mary Jo and Jay Mooncotch, Brian Schwammlein, Johnny McAuley, Nate Kingsbury, Amos Gray, Tony Schwartz, Lynette Rubin, and Curtis McFarland. Thank you all for your help. Special thanks to Dave Whiting, Darren DeGraaf, and Mike Lueth, who gave above and beyond to review our manuscript and who brought their wisdom and learning to make this a better tool. Last but not least, Christine Anderson brought her enthusiastic realism to this project and kept us on task, focusing our meandering chatter so it could become coherent words on a page. "Very interesting, guys, but getting back to the mentoring book ..." Christine, this project would not have started—or finished—without your help. Thanks for sharing your gifts with us.

And now, while the window of opportunity for this generation is still open, turn the page ... and get ready to change a student's life—and your life—forever.

chapter 1

A Frame of Mind

If it matters, it's measured. In business, it's profit. In politics, it's votes. In sports, it's points. If you're reading this book, you're among those of us from all walks of life who care about the spiritual development of students. You might be a volunteer, a parent, a professional youth worker, or a pastor. How do you measure effectiveness in what you do with students? Is it attendance at weekly meetings? Is it the number of students in small groups? Is it how many kids go to camp? How many kids get baptized? How few students you lost over the course of the year compared to last year's attrition? Do you count letters of appreciation from students, their parents, or your senior pastor?

By those kinds of measures you might feel pretty good at the end of a ministry season. You might not. But what do you really know about your ministry if you *only* pay attention to easily measured externals? When you check in with your own heart at the end of the ministry season, how do you feel deep down inside about what you've accomplished—and what it took out of you to accomplish it? There may have been a huge cost to your family, or outside friendships may have suffered. *Was it worth it?*

the payoff

I (Bo) have been working with students in full-time ministry for over twenty years. I've taught other leaders about vision and building prevailing youth ministries, strategic planning, developing teams, organizing large events—and at one time led one of the largest student ministries in the country. Despite all the rewards that came from this, I return again and again in my mind to two questions: *What really matters? Am I successful in God's sight?*

Let me take you back to my early ministry years. When I first started out in youth ministry, I was twenty-seven, a new Christian, and knew very little about what I was doing. I'd been a football coach, but then God called me into full-time ministry. In my first few years of leading students, I learned so much. I learned one of the most important lessons about what really matters while sitting on a brick wall in a Burbank, California church parking lot.

Every Tuesday night we held a high school outreach event at our church. We worked hard to provide a quality program where Christian students could invite their non-Christian friends to hear the message of Christ. Several hundred high school students came for an evening of sports activities and a program that featured drama, a live band, and a message. We never knew what to expect or what God might do.

After the program was over, the leadership team—about twelve high school and college students—gathered in a certain spot in the parking lot. It wasn't a planned meeting, but we always seemed to spontaneously show up there—sitting on a low brick wall. At first there'd be a lot of people—students who came for the first time, or regulars who stopped by to say hi or to introduce a friend. At some point, all the students said good-night and I'd be standing there with just the guys I was mentoring: Coleman, Dave, Troy, Trevor, and Alex. The six of us were always the last to leave. And that's when the storytelling would begin.

There were all sorts of stories—both funny and touching. We laughed about what went wrong that night, how bad the music was, mistakes in the drama, something I said in the message that didn't make sense, or something that happened during the sports competition. Then the mood changed and the stories shifted from the activities of the evening to the people whose lives were being changed. One of my guys had been praying for months that a friend would come, and he shared how the friend finally showed up for the first time—and loved it. Some had conversations with friends about God, and right then and there God had begun to change their lives. Others had friends who showed signs of wanting to know more about God. And then there were those fantastic celebrations when we found out one of the students had prayed to receive Christ.

I remember looking at these guys, listening to their stories, and thinking, *This is what I want to give my life to. This is what really matters to me.* I had an incredible sense of fulfillment when I looked into the eyes of these students and saw their compassion, their commitment, and their love for God. Right there in that empty parking lot, sitting on that brick wall, God showed me what ministry was all about. That is why I worked so hard and what allowed me to get through all the other "stuff" that has to be done in youth ministry—those times were the payoff.

When we finally said good-bye and climbed into our cars to head home, I always left with an overwhelming sense of gratitude in my spirit. Although I was tired from the evening, I also had new energy and passion for ministry because I knew these guys and I believed in them. And, twenty-some years later, I still love "sitting on the brick wall," looking into the eyes of a few high school students I know and love well, seeing their passion, their desire, and their ambition to change the world.

was Jesus a success?

Imagine for a minute how we might measure the effectiveness of Jesus' ministry while he was here on earth. Granted, he drew some large crowds at the height of his popularity. But only 120 were gathered in the upper room a few weeks after his death—not the several hundreds who'd cheered his triumphal entry into Jerusalem or the thousands who'd flocked to hear him on the hillsides. Where did they all go? And what about the senior spiritual leaders of his day who almost universally opposed him, his message, and his methods? A snapshot taken just before Pentecost looks like a ministry in decline, if not dead in the water—not a movement that would shake up the world.

Despite all this apparent "failure," Jesus unblinkingly proclaimed that he'd completed what the Father sent him to do (John 17:4). So by Jesus' measure of success (whatever it was), he'd made it. He said he'd accomplished all his goals.

What explains this discrepancy? How can his ministry results seem so paltry by one set of criteria, yet he be so satisfied and at peace with his accomplishments? We believe we can find the answer by reflecting on Jesus' ministry using a different plumb line (Amos 7:7). We need to re-evaluate our definitions of success and instead take a close look at the depth of impact he made on a few key individuals.

Jesus' impact was one of personal transformation deep within the souls of those he touched. These men and women he spent time with found their lives radically altered, even without their full understanding of how or to what extent. Yet as the months and years went by, they discovered just how deep and permanent the "Jesus impact" had been.

Let's return to the days just after Jesus' earthly ministry ended. We find Mary Magdalene, released from demonic bondage, who became the first messenger of Jesus' resurrection. And Peter, though waffling in a time of testing, came back and powerfully preached before thousands. Philip was part of a revival in Samaria soon after the resurrection and even led a visiting Ethiopian official to faith in Christ. John boldly proclaimed Jesus, suffering multiple arrests and enduring a flogging with joy. All the other original Twelve (with the exception of Judas) became fruitful servants of the new Jesus movement in the face of rejection and persecution — most paying with their lives.

Jesus *was* a success despite his dismal numbers, because the measurement that mattered wasn't just a short-term body count. We believe the standard by which Jesus measured his own success — and how we also ought to measure our success — was *deep, lasting change in a few*. As Dallas Willard has suggested, Christians must be weighed, not just counted.[1] Jesus' public notoriety had very little to do with the more enduring effect he had on that rag-tag band of average Joes and Sallys — and the subsequent effect (through the power of the Holy Spirit) they, not the masses, had on the world. Jesus' life and teaching so altered them that they gave the rest of their natural lives to perpetuating his work. In an age like ours where it seems a large percent of churched high school students are no longer connected to any church within a few years after college, wouldn't results like those be a refreshing change?

---

1. Dallas Willard and Dieter Zander, "The Apprentices" *Leadership Journal*, (Summer 2005). *www.christianitytoday.com/le/2005/003/2.20.html.*

Deep transformation of a few who continue to influence others is the measure we invite you to embrace. And the one word that best captures how to accomplish this is *mentoring*. There is little doubt Jesus' methodology worked, because here you are, his follower twenty centuries later, desiring to lead others to be more like him. A fully-orbed youth ministry can't be reduced to just one simple word, but no healthy youth ministry can exist without the strategic, intentional development of young followers of Jesus Christ. The fact you're reading this book suggests you're willing to consider your role. And our prayer is that God would confirm that calling by the time you finish.

Jesus measured what mattered and he gave his life to make lasting change happen. We who are his followers are wise to do the same. And the good news is, we can!

ministry large and small

The simple truth is that Jesus had it right. His focus was always on relationships, and his ministry was in perfect balance: he gathered and spoke to crowds but never allowed their size or adulation trick him into thinking he had done his work. Rather, while speaking and ministering to the many, he also found a few young men and women to invest in deeply, and with the power of the Holy Spirit, that band of followers "turned the world upside down" (Acts 17:6 NLT). This generation needs that to happen again.

We believe that students are waiting for someone to show them the way. That's what makes youth ministry so exciting—you get to invest in a few young difference-makers just like Jesus did. What a privilege to be a part of forming young lives!

Let's go back to the beginning of Jesus' ministry. It didn't take long for him to attract a loose following and call some specific people to join his movement. But in Mark 3, he takes his relational involvement a huge step further. After spending a night in prayer, we read that he gathered a select few and appointed them to "be with him" (Mark 3:14). Jesus selected twelve, and we know there were a few others in this inner circle, including at least three women (Luke 8:1–3). Though public miracles and teaching would be the most obvious aspect of his ministry, he would accomplish the deep work among the few who followed him day in and day out. Walking from town to town, handling the crowds, laughing, eating, sleeping, serving—all parts of daily life would be the training ground for their transformation.

We know from history that it was common for a Jewish teacher (called a rabbi) to gather around himself a small cluster of people who became known as his disciples (the word means "learners"). Jesus used a similar technique of close association in daily life to teach his young disciples. He knew the power of modeling. He knew it would take more than a classroom, books, or conferences—more than thirty minutes of training a week—to transform his followers into his image and set in motion a new world movement. It would take "being-with" a few and intentionally building into them over time for his work to be established.

So at the heart of any ministry that seeks to emulate Jesus—no matter how expansive or public its outward manifestation may be—there must be a commitment from the leaders to mentor a few in the daily aspects of living. We call that the Be-With Factor. Jesus lived it, and it's God's call on everyone who follows in Jesus' steps. We will say it again: for anyone who cares about students, mentoring is by far the most rewarding activity to engage in. No question, youth ministry is hard work. But trust us, it will become much harder if you lose your passion. If you neglect to "be-with" a few students where life-change really happens, your zeal will cool. You cannot afford to watch lives change from a distance. Mentoring gets you up close. *Whatever else you do, "be-with" a few so that lasting life-change happens.*

the Bible and the be-with pattern

We don't find the Be-With pattern just with Jesus. We see it at work throughout Scripture. Other leaders in God's kingdom made similar relational investments. Consider the example of Moses. He led a huge nation and invested in young Joshua, Caleb, and Aaron, and then he passed the baton of national leadership to Joshua. Or Elijah, a prophet of God, called Elisha to "be-with" him as his attendant, and Elisha carried on that prophetic legacy with a "double portion" of Elijah's spiritual power (2 Kings 2:9). Paul mentored young Timothy and Titus; Paul's words to Timothy are foundational to the Be-With model: "And the things you have heard me say in the presence of many witnesses entrust to reliable men who will also be qualified to teach others" (2 Tim. 2:2). Paul's legacy helped those men and others to have fruitful ministries, and he left behind writings that are essentially his mentoring notes, which still encourage leaders to this day.

Looking up from the pages of Scripture and looking out at the state of our postmodern world, the need for mentoring is even more apparent. Skyrocketing divorce rates and lack of stable adult role models make it even more imperative that those of us who care about youth in the name of Jesus seriously engage in the intentional development of a few potential leaders through mentoring. As a mentor, you can play a major role in turning around the destructive trend that threatens a whole generation, and you'll help raise up a cadre of leaders to take the church into the challenges and opportunities of the twenty-first century. Isn't that worth giving your life to—and what youth ministry should be all about?

a picture of mentoring

What exactly does mentoring look like in today's world? In its simplest form, mentoring is "being-with" in daily life. It's not just a formal small group time or giving the student lessons from a planned syllabus. It's spending time with individual students, taking them along with you as you go about some of your daily tasks—or accompanying them while they do theirs. In those experiences, common and everyday as they are, you keep an eye on them and an ear tuned to the promptings of the Holy Spirit. They watch you and learn how a maturing believer does life (presumably, you *are* maturing!). They also watch your mistakes; those, too, form learning laboratories. From your missteps they learn how someone owns their failures and makes wrongs right, how a person can admit faults and be okay with that, and how to be humble about being a "work in progress" rather than someone who has it all together. Sometimes the focus is on them and you comment on what you see. Other times they ask questions about what they see in you. Those words and experiences, combined with God's truths, supply them with a roadmap for how to walk with God and be the difference-makers he's called them to be.

a way of life

Mentoring is not primarily another "to do" on your weekly agenda. It can become a natural part of your lifestyle. Mentoring is going through your existing agenda while a student is there with you, sometimes simply shadowing you, watching you in meetings, or listening to you talk. At other times, you're in a more interactive role: serving, teaching, or doing ministry together. While there will be formal meeting times with those you are mentoring, the real defining moments happen in the unplanned discussions and spontaneous learning experiences. Unforeseen circumstances are often the very place where the most profound "aha" lights go on for the student, or where you as the mentor make your most life-changing observations. In short, mentoring is where the Christian life is *caught*, not *taught*.

Recently, I (Bo) heard from Ronnie, a leader I mentored a few years ago. Let me share with you what he said:

> Bo, check this out—the ministry has grown to over a hundred students. I've already found the two guys I need to invest in: John and Hunter. I meet with them one-on-one each week to challenge, teach, and pray with them. Does that sound familiar? But I know this is not where mentoring takes place. What's cool is that I really am deeply a part of these guys' lives, and they are already deeply a part of mine. I take them with me on appointments with other students, have them over to my house to watch football, and give them input in ministry decisions as well as leadership roles to fill. It's so much fun. I have only been working with them for six months, and it's already amazing to see what God is doing through our relationship. Both of these guys have already become so involved in our ministry, really discovering what their spiritual gifts are and leading in a big way. I also see their passion for reaching their friends increasing. The coolest thing of all is that they already want to mentor a few guys themselves. Second Timothy 2:2 ... it's happening in my life now. Thanks, Bo, for teaching me the importance of mentoring. What's really cool is that it's not just happening up there in Chicago, but it's alive and well here in Alabama as well ... and it all goes back to you showing me the Be-With Factor through your example.

Ann is also a leader who understands mentoring as a lifestyle. I was able to work with her years ago when she was interning for me, and now she's continuing to make a difference as a youth pastor in Virginia.

During my first year at my current ministry, I had my hands full and my calendar packed with all I needed to do to learn about my new church and the ministry I was now in charge of leading. I met with a few students here and there, but I didn't think I had enough time or energy to actually mentor any single student. Bo, I know, I know — you're saying, "It's a lifestyle, it's not supposed to make your life crazy but get folded into your existing schedule." Keep reading!

One of the students, a junior in high school at the time, had shown a lot of leadership potential, so I met with her over the summer to talk about leading a small group of middle school students. While meeting with her, I realized, prompted by the Spirit, that this was a girl I needed to be more intentional with despite feeling my calendar was already packed. So we began a mentoring relationship. We met at least once a week over bagels and Diet Coke, we took walks, ran errands together, served together on Sunday nights, and basically just lived life together. She became not only a student that I mentored but a friend that I served alongside of.

We started talking about her gifts and worked specifically to develop them. She overcame huge barriers, and as I saw her step out of her comfort zone time and time again, I was amazed at this young woman's serious desire to follow and serve Jesus. For example, I eventually met all of her non-Christian friends and together we led a sort of "seeker small group" with them. After we started this, and after she had spoken up front a number of times, she shared with me that she used to stutter every time she spoke in a group, even if it was only three or four people. She told me she had decided to say yes to all my challenges and ask God for the strength and courage to serve in whatever way she could. She went on to say that she never stuttered since the first time she said yes.

I was so honored to have been a part of her journey and to watch her grow like a weed, overcome huge barriers, and make a difference in the kingdom. It was, hands down, the most energizing part of my week. Once I started mentoring, not only did I find the time but I realized that mentoring was the heart of what God had called me to do.

not best friends

Mentoring is not the same as peer-to-peer friendships. While mentoring is friendly, the mentor is not just a friend. Mentoring is not parenting and it's not therapy either. A mentor is someone with a measure of maturity, life experience, and age that exceeds the student's — maybe by only a few years—willing to build into and model life for a student. Ideally, a mentor is an adult (over twenty-one) and the student is in middle or high school (twelve to eighteen years of age). At a minimum, a mentor must be at least one "life-stage" ahead of the student.

One clarification: sometimes in a business setting, people speak of "finding a mentor." That person usually has a specific expertise, and the mentoring centers around skill development. When you mentor a student, however, you are more of a "life generalist" than someone with specific expertise. The scope of what you could talk about extends to virtually any area of life.

not looking for quick results

There are several other aspects of a mentoring mind-set. A good mentor knows that the investment in a student won't necessarily pay off in the short-term, but he or she does not become discouraged. The reason that lack of immediate results is acceptable is because the mentor looks at the bigger picture—the long-term view of life-change—and is content to "plant a shade tree under which someone else will sit." A good mentor also knows not to worry about having every detail planned out when meeting with the student; she is ready for anything and able to respond to the need of the moment. A mentor shares what is going on in her life—her own experiences and times with God—giving "new treasures as well as old" to the student (Matt. 13:52). And a mentor knows that "it is more blessed to give than to receive" (Acts 20:35); giving to the student is more than matched by the student returning energy and enthusiasm to what the mentor is trying to do throughout all of her ministry.

That last point is especially important for youth pastors to grasp. In the midst of a busy ministry schedule, mentoring can seem like an impossible demand, like trying to shoehorn one more draining experience into an already dangerously overbooked calendar. But in reality, mentoring is a refueling and revitalizing endeavor. It keeps you in the game and keeps on fire your zeal for the work. At the end of a ministry season, being able to see a student or two who have actually grown and changed in a deep way is the very reward that helps you say yes to another year of putting your hand to the plow. Shepherding the whole youth group has its own reward, but mentoring one or two students can make the difference between quitting or staying, between indifference or loving those you lead. And over a lifetime, there's nothing more satisfying than seeing a trail of students that you've invested in continue to leave their mark in the lives of those around them.

Dave was a seventeen-year-old kid when I (Bo) first met him. I was so impressed with his brightness and his heart to know God's Word. Dave is a grown man now and has his Master of Divinity degree. It was so cool to hear what he remembered most about our mentoring relationship:

> With you and me, it was "a burrito and a Coke." Some of the best times we had together were eating out or talking in the parking lot after church. You taking time to just chat made a big difference in my life. It's the cumulative effect of many months of casual time spent together that's made an impact; your ideas, values, and priorities were conveyed in everyday conversation.
>
> I remember you being vulnerable to admit when things got goofed up during a ministry event. Your philosophy of "we'll laugh about this later" made ministry much easier to handle. It helped knowing you weren't holding a stick over us, waiting to whack us upside the head. Just living through the glitches together enabled us to see you under pressure and to see the fruit of the Spirit—or the growth that was still needed.
>
> Of course, there were "formal" times of teaching, exhortation, correction, etc. But it's the personal touches, the one-on-one times that remain in my memory the most.
>
> I think of how the disciples, years after Jesus ascended to heaven, must have remembered the personal times with him, the little things he said and did, and cringed at the mistakes they made, laughing about the glitches. Maybe what they missed most were the "burrito and Coke" moments.

the right measures

At the beginning of this chapter we talked about what people measure in life. Student ministry isn't a job, a political office to run for, or an athletic competition. Sales, votes, and points don't count with God. But here's what does matter and what a mentor measures: Christ-like change in the life of a few students. We know that you want to see this happen. That's why the challenge for you to become a mentor is so important. That's what mentors long for, and they order their lives to bring it to pass. Mentors adopt this mind-set because they hear the commendation of the One whose example they follow, and they feel the satisfaction of a life well invested. They leave a legacy, and it has a young person's name on it.

Our question is, *What are you leaving?* Why not stop to pray right now, asking God to show you who you need to "be-with"? Who are the few you need to invest your life in? Think about the names of two students as you read the rest of this book and ask God to give you the mind-set of a mentor. Building your legacy starts now.

The Real World ...

After reading each chapter, we anticipate you might be wondering how all this relates to you. Maybe you're still in the dark about something, or you might feel some frustration that we don't seem to understand your situation. Some of the folks in the trenches of youth ministry who read our early drafts *did* ask us pointed questions. At the close of each chapter, we're going to take their questions—and others you might be asking—and see if we can give some quick responses to clear up any lingering confusion.

Great concept, sounds worthwhile, but you just don't understand my life. I don't have time for what I'm already doing, let alone trying to mentor someone.

We understand busyness, we really do. But if you are in full-time ministry, there's no substitute for modeling what you want all your other leaders to do—and that is to produce life-change. Mentoring is the most effective way to do that. And remember, we're encouraging you to do this as a part of your life (we'll unpack this in more detail later)—not to add many more meetings and activities. In some ways, this is the simplest thing you'll do in a week; just hang out with a student while you do what you were going to do anyway.

And if you are a volunteer, the same applies; just take a student along with you as you go through life. We promise, you won't believe how much it will fuel you to have this kind of relationship.

I'm a youth pastor, and I'm evaluated on the very numbers you were so disparagingly talking about. What do I do?

A good idea might be to have those who evaluate you read this book. It will help them see your heart. Remember, mentoring will not take away from doing your job—instead it will add to your ministry and your life in so many positive ways. Our claim is that this has to be a lifestyle choice; in time, church leaders (and for that matter, your entire team) will see that this is a part of your life. They will soon witness the benefits in the lives of the students, as well as the benefits that come back to you as the leader. And this is also true for those of you volunteering in a youth ministry. We know there's only so much you can do. But keep serving. Keep sharing your life. By having a student next to you and by just living life with them, you are giving a huge gift. And you'll be surprised by how much it gives back to you as well.

I lead a very small ministry with no help. How am I supposed to mentor? [Or] I lead a very large ministry with lots of volunteers. How am I supposed to mentor?

We've found that ministry size has very little to do with whether or not you can mentor. The value of mentoring is the same, whether your ministry is large, small, or somewhere in between. We have many testimonies from youth pastors and volunteers from every conceivable size ministry, and the uniform witness is that once you commit to this as a lifestyle, it energizes you rather than drains you. Those who mentor and those who don't have virtually the same pressures time-wise. In other words, this commitment shouldn't make your life any harder; there's a good chance you'll be blessed, enriched, and energized by becoming a mentor.

I lead leaders, not students. Isn't that how Jesus did his ministry—investing in the leaders rather than taking care of everybody?

Really, Jesus did it all. He taught the masses, worked with his disciples, healed individuals, loved little kids ... he had a fully-orbed ministry, and so should you. As a leader, you need to invest in both leaders and students. Be careful not to isolate yourself from the very people you want to serve (students). A close relationship with a few students will serve you well—and should not take away from the important investment in the leaders in your ministry. And we believe that your leaders will respect you more if you are in the trenches with them and have some real-life stories of what you're experiencing with students. Trust us ... you will love it. And we believe it will give you more leadership capacity, not less.

chapter summary

Verse to Remember: 1 Thessalonians 2:8

We loved you so much that we were delighted to share with you not only the gospel of God but our lives as well, because you had become so dear to us.

The standard by which Jesus measured his own ministry success, and how we ought to measure our success, was deep, lasting change in a few. And one word that captures a great way to accomplish that change is "mentoring." In its simplest form, mentoring is being-with a student in daily life. Mentoring is not primarily another "to do" on your weekly agenda, but rather becomes a natural part of your lifestyle. As a mentor of a young student, you can play a major role in turning around the destructive trend that threatens a whole generation and help raise up a cadre of leaders to take the church into the twenty-first century.

chapter 2

A Guiding Strategy

The English word *strategy* comes from the Greek word for a military general. The basic definition of *strategy* is related to warfare—"the planning and methodology employed by a general to win a war."

it's a war out there

As a mentor, you are a general in an army that is fighting for the student's well-being and future. It's not an exaggeration to say that at times, mentoring mounts a counterattack on the Devil himself, who targets not only the student but all the potential good that a young person might do in the world. We do not fight this war alone; we coordinate with others (parents, teachers, pastors, and friends) and most importantly, we teach the student to put on all God's armor, and we fight alongside them when the battles come. There are no prisoners in this war. The stakes are high—and it's a winner-takes-all deal. As a mentor, you need to be in this fight to *win*.

When it comes to mentoring, what exactly *is* the war? And how does mentoring help win it? We believe there is a war going on for the soul and maturity of every student. The apostle Paul described his ministry goals using a military metaphor. His words are appropriate for mentors as well: "We use our powerful God-tools [weapons] for smashing warped philosophies, tearing down barriers erected against the truth of God, fitting every loose thought and emotion and impulse into the structure of life shaped by Christ" (2 Cor. 10:5 MSG). Mentors come alongside students to model how they do this in their own lives and then help the students win their own battles.

The fight is not necessarily dramatic. Some of the enemies are simply ignorance or lack of life experience. Some of the foes are external influences that will mislead the student. Some are internal immaturities that keep the student stuck. Some of the adversaries are evil forces at work in our world, unseen, but real and destructive; they require perseverate prayer and continued spiritual resistance.

> For we are not fighting against people made of flesh and blood, but against the evil rulers and authorities of the unseen world, against those mighty powers of darkness who rule this world, and against wicked spirits in the heavenly realms.... Stand your ground, putting on the sturdy belt of truth and the body armor of God's righteousness. For shoes, put on the peace that comes from the Good News ... In every battle you will need faith as your shield ... Put on salvation as your helmet, and take the sword of the Spirit, which is the word of God. Pray at all times and on every occasion in the power of the Holy Spirit. Stay alert and be persistent in your prayers.
> EPH. 6:12, 14–18 NLT

Simply put, we must "resist the devil, and he will flee from [us]" (James 4:7). We must do this for both ourselves and the next generation.

an intentional strategy

What is the mentoring strategy? How do we win the war over everything that stands in the way of a student growing to Christ-like maturity? If there is one key word to keep in mind, it is the word "intention." A mentoring relationship is an intentional relationship. All the activities you engage in come back to this one principle: your intention is to help the student grow, and that intention guides you to select the activities and words that comprise your mentoring experience. You know what you're trying to do, and you determine to find ways to help the student.

Mentoring must be real. There is no point in being fake or phony. You cannot try to make yourself look better than you are. And the things you talk about with your student must ring true. They must relate to real life as the student experiences it — not some well-scrubbed, artificial spiritual hokum. There may be some teaching, but you're not a Sunday school teacher. The student may be a pupil, but you are not in a classroom.

If Jesus had said in his Great Commission, "Teach them everything I have commanded you," classrooms would suffice to get the job done. But he said, "[Teach] them *to obey* everything I have commanded you" (Matt. 28:20, emphasis added). Classrooms, weekly programs, and Sunday schools are not enough for that to happen. Obedience is learned in the school of life. It will require mentoring.

practical joke, practical lesson

It was late Friday night and I (Bo) was tired. We'd had a great time at the youth ministry party, but my wife, Gloria, and I were ready to go home. As we said good-night and walked out the door, I saw Chris smiling and watching me in a way that gave me the impression he was up to something.

I'd mentored Chris for about two years. He was seventeen, a natural leader, and had a fun edge to him that I really liked. His peers looked up to him, and he was definitely an influence on his high school campus. Chris was always joking around, which was sometimes a problem. Though he was outrageously funny, at times he didn't know when to stop. More than once I'd seen his practical jokes hurt people.

"Hey, have a great night, Bo," Chris yelled across the room. "Enjoy your ride home." I turned and gave Chris a "you better not mess with me" look as I walked out the door. My first thought was *I bet that little sucker put toilet paper around my car.* I was sort of right. When we got to the car, I saw only a couple sheets of toilet paper. I relaxed and thought, *He knew better than to mess with me.*

When Gloria and I pulled into our driveway, I noticed a few more strands of toilet paper hanging from the tree in the front yard. *Pretty good, Chris, but you were smart not to go too far.* As we got out of the car and walked to the front porch, we both noticed a strand of toilet paper around the doorknob. My wife gave me a horrified look. When I opened the door, all we could see was a giant spiderweb of white.

There was toilet paper everywhere—and I mean *everywhere*. I started to laugh, but Gloria was on the verge of tears.

Chris and two of his friends had actually duplicated my house key and used over two hundred rolls of toilet paper inside our home. Yes, two hundred rolls. It took us over an hour to pick up enough just to be able to walk through the house.

While we were cleaning up, the phone rang. I dug through the web and found the phone. "Hey, Bo, hope you're enjoying your little present," said Chris in a cocky, "what do you think of me now?" tone.

My wife's anger and sadness made me realize I needed to speak some hard truth to Chris. "I'll be by your house tomorrow morning at eight o'clock to pick you up. Be ready. We need to talk."

"Hey Bo, are you okay?" Chris asked. "Are you mad?"

"It's late. We'll talk in the morning," I replied.

The next morning on the drive to Chris' house, I thought about what I could do to set a better example for him. You see, I believed that in a way, I'd brought this on myself. I hadn't helped him understand appropriate behavior. I thought about the kidding around we did—the times we had both joined in on practical jokes. I realized I had set the wrong example. I knew I had to speak truth to Chris—both about what he'd done wrong, as well as what I'd done wrong.

I picked him up and we went out for a cup of coffee. I spoke honestly from the heart about my anger and disappointment. Though I'd had a brief laugh when I opened the door, he had violated my home and my family by invading our privacy. When he duplicated our house key and toilet-papered everything, including our bedroom, he'd broken our trust. I told him he'd gone too far, and he owed us an apology. He immediately owned up, said he was sorry, and offered to do whatever he could to make it right. I told him he could start by apologizing to Gloria.

Then I apologized to Chris. I told him I was sorry I hadn't set a good example for him. And I extended a challenge to both Chris and myself—a challenge we would do together: I wanted us to change the way we looked at having fun. Instead of practical jokes, we would look for opportunities to serve people in radical, creative ways—to help rather than hurt, embarrass, or make fun of them.

As we finished our coffee that morning, I once again realized how important my example was in this mentoring relationship. Even as we began to brainstorm about creative ways we could help other people,

I sensed a whole new depth of relationship. There was a different feel to our conversation, and I knew he was getting on the right track. He would also grow by apologizing to Gloria, and I felt good about the way I'd modeled how a husband respects, cares for, and stands up for his wife. Chris' practical joke was turning into a series of practical lessons, and the classroom was life itself.

God's strategy for making adults

The main formative relationship that exists between human beings is the parent-child relationship. And one of God's key strategies in that training program is found in Deuteronomy 6:6–7. "These commandments that I give you today are to be upon your hearts. Impress them on your children. Talk about them when you sit at home and when you walk along the road, when you lie down and when you get up." No mention of a classroom there. On the contrary, the setting is daily life. Every place in life is a learning opportunity when character and values are the curriculum: sitting around the house, walking somewhere, getting ready for bed—and over a cup of coffee in the morning after a practical joke goes too far. It's as if God says, "Do you want your kids to share your values—the values I gave you? Then they'll have to see those values folded into your life so consistently that no matter what you do, they come pouring out of you."

Mentoring is not parenting—let's be clear about that. But in some respects, it utilizes this same "when-you-sit-at-home-when-you-walk-along-the-road" method God gave to parents. Mentoring can reinforce what good parents do, using similar tools such as love, modeling, listening, feedback, and meaningful contact in a variety of life-contexts.

Here are some other helpful distinctions:

A mentor is not a tutor. A tutor is an expert in one subject and helps the student learn that subject. But a mentor's scope is much wider, and more about life in general.

A mentor is not a professional counselor. A student with a sustained emotional problem should not only look to a mentor for help but also seek a qualified Christian counselor.

A mentor is not a teacher. You're not an instructor in a classroom, and the goal is not to help a student master some body of material. Mentors work through life, not books.

A mentor isn't a small group leader or shepherd, though they could participate in this ministry as well. Small group leaders have more students (usually four to ten) based around curriculum or a book study. A shepherd's care usually extends beyond the one to three students that a mentor cares for, and is usually not as in-depth as a mentoring relationship. Also, shepherds can be peer-to-peer rather than adult-to-student.

Mentoring is not the same as discipling. This distinction is perhaps the hardest to make, partly because various Christians define the phrase "to disciple" so differently, and partly because there *is* considerable overlap no matter how it's defined. Because of all the baggage and confusion, we prefer to use the term "mentoring" to describe what we're doing, even though some people reading this book will say we are promoting basic discipleship. Most discipling literature we've seen stresses the use of a curriculum to help build Christian character or spiritual disciplines. The emphasis in mentoring is more on the Be-With aspect, not a curriculum (even if one is used).

Jesus' strategy

Jesus wanted life-change to happen to those who followed him. How did he expect that to occur? Did he think he could just talk to his followers and they'd be transformed? Did he zap them with instant spiritual power or maturity? Did he pass out a manual for Christian behavior and ask them to master it? Did he start a conference or plan some big weekend event? Did he enroll them in a local Christian school and check back periodically to monitor their progress?

Let's read it again, right from the pages of Scripture: "Then Jesus went up on a mountain and called to him the men he wanted, and they came to him. Jesus chose twelve men and called them apostles. He wanted them to be with him" (Mark 3:13–14 NCV). To make them ready, they would ... *do what?* The text is clear: *be with* him.

Those words "be with" jump off the page. They had profound importance for the ones he chose. They have profound importance for us. "Being-with" is the heart of Jesus' program for turning fishermen into fishers of men. We can see from Deuteronomy 6 that this act is at the heart of turning children into spiritually vital adults. That is why students need mentors, and why—as mentors—we need to recognize mentoring is at the heart of helping students grow into their full redemptive potential. The Be-With model is the mentor's edge. It's the battle plan. It's how we win the war.

Think about what being with Jesus must have been like for the disciples. They were able to observe Jesus in every conceivable setting. They were awed by his miracle-working abilities but also touched by his personal responsiveness to them. They watched and listened as he taught the expectant crowds, but then he took time to talk with them personally when the crowds had gone away. Walking between towns, the conversation must have covered every conceivable topic. They went to weddings, funerals, and dinner parties together—and many of the stories of these shared events are recorded in Scripture for our benefit as well. The disciples watched Jesus eat, sleep, and do everything in between. It was very unique and personal.

Think about the impact on their lives when he took that kind of time with them and spoke such personal words to them. What a difference between talking *about* the need to love and serve others—which no doubt the disciples had heard preached at their local synagogues since they were children—and Jesus washing their feet to illustrate that kind of love in action. The water on their feet, Jesus' rough hands holding the towel, his knees bent in humble servanthood before them ... I am sure every disciple carried that image and the bodily sensations of that moment for the rest of their lives. His teachings and stories were of course magnificent lessons that left an impression, but the personal interaction Jesus had with his closest followers surely changed their souls at a core level.

Jesus' training program also included ministry assignments. On several occasions he sent them away in pairs on short trips to practice what they'd learned. Imagine the conversations around the campfire the night they came back! From what the Gospels tell us, they talked about how amazed they were at what God had done. Then Jesus gave them feedback—specific words that both encouraged and challenged them, personally and theologically (Luke 10:17–24). They got a chance to put into practice the Be-With lessons he taught them, and then were able to "be-with" him for a debriefing session and the next level of teaching.

Can you start to see the impact you will have on a few students using Jesus' Be-With plan? Can you see how students will be better prepared to fight the battles they're in? Can you see how this plan can win a generation of young leaders that will change the world? We pray that you do.

twenty-first century implementation

Mentors in our day translate Jesus' example into times of teaching, then releasing students into ministry, followed by evaluation to help them learn from their experiences. In the midst of that, we carve out times to be together with students often, and we wait expectantly for God to show up. Even if there is no great breakthrough or unforgettable connection, mentors continue to be an example. Hard as that may be, they don't give in to discouragement, trusting the process to do its work over time.

Naturally, a mentor has to fulfill daily responsibilities such as work and family obligations. But as a mentor, "being-with" means opening your life, allowing a student or two to tag along, sharing insights, observations, or just being together without saying anything. Sometimes, the mentor chooses a special mentoring activity: grabbing a meal, attending a sporting event, hiking or biking together, or some other such meeting. Most of the time what's done together is an activity that would be done anyway, yet with the students there.

For example, you can take a student with you when you go shopping. Or, if you have to do a project around the house or work on your car, do it with the student. If you're a runner, jog together. If you're a biker, bike together. If you have to drive around doing errands, take the student along and talk as you drive. If you have children, take the student along when you fulfill some of your parenting responsibilities (with the caveat that you shouldn't cheat your kids out of their time alone with you). Maybe invite the student to shadow you for part of your workday, or when you fulfill some other volunteer responsibility that doesn't directly involve the student, but gives them an opportunity to watch you in action. Have the student join you when you are with some of your adult friends. Although you don't have live-in disciples like Jesus had, you can still have a powerful impact by coming up with a variety of settings in which to be together, and because this can be part of your lifestyle, it should not be a burden. Remember, this is not extra work. It's not more time away from your loved ones or family. It's not time taken away from your need to be alone. It's time shared in the flow of life that you are going to live out anyway. The difference is that you choose to "be-with" a few, just like Jesus did. You can do this.

Here's how Be-With time might play out on a typical week:

Personal	Have a student join you at the club for a workout session on Monday.
Ministry	Have a student sit in on a planning meeting with you Tuesday after school.
Devotional	Pray with a student and other leaders before a ministry event Wednesday night.
Family	Have a student join you and your family for a Saturday BBQ.

You wouldn't do this much with one student in one week; this could be a plan for connecting with two or three students, or it could be an example of Be-With times with one student over a few weeks. Notice that you haven't done anything differently that week than you would have done anyway. You've just included a student in some of your activities; you've adjusted your lifestyle, not your calendar.

mentoring benefits youth pastors and volunteers

If you're a youth pastor or leader, it's probably difficult for you to imagine how you can preach, teach, and lead the whole ministry well without personal, in-depth, ongoing contact with a few students (not just the group). Mentoring is a great way to have that contact. Obviously, your goal should be to reach the maximum number of students with the gospel message, and we know how easy it is to focus on the metrics you track of building and growing the ministry. It can be overwhelming at times. When students come to your group meetings in increasing numbers, you want them to grow in their faith and become mature followers of Christ who will impact their world for him. You run youth programs to reach and teach the most students possible. But even as you're doing that group work, when you are mentoring a student as well, you get important insights into the lives of students that you wouldn't have ministering just to groups. Naturally, you must protect the privacy of the students you mentor—if you are a teacher, it would not be appropriate to use that student's life struggles as a ready source of illustrations in your public talks. But the insight you gain from close association can translate into speaking with a great deal more understanding, compassion, and accuracy, which increases your credibility with the audience.

We know the pressures you can face as a youth leader, and how important it is to build a leadership team. But you must strike a balance to be really effective. Sometimes youth leaders get into the odd conundrum of spending so much time with leaders or other youth pastors, they hardly spend any meaningful time with students—the very reason they went into ministry. If you're a youth leader, guard against that tendency to get further and further away from personal interaction with the generation you're in ministry to change.

As a leader, you need to equip and empower other leaders. I (Bo) personally love to lead and coach leaders of leaders. I love to influence and invest in young leaders. But we must stay connected to students if we really want to be as effective as possible. I believe this is what has personally kept me in the game for over twenty years. Use the gift God has given you to lead and influence, but make sure you stay connected to what God has ultimately called you to—investing in students' lives.

Whether you are a full-time youth pastor or a volunteer, mentoring benefits your ministry in other ways as well. Mentoring increases your overall passion for ministry. There's just something about what goes on in that relationship that we believe pleases God and fuels your fire and passion for youth ministry in general. The students you mentor tend to be "owners" in the youth ministry, and exert a positive influence on other students. It's also a great way to keep upperclassmen involved, who tend to drift as they see the finish line of high school coming. By mentoring an upperclassman, not only will *that* student stay involved, they will tend to keep their junior and senior friends involved.

Another indirect benefit of mentoring is the way it impacts other ministry volunteers. They are watching you too and can tell if you're a mere theoretician who's read all the right books and studied the commentaries but hasn't connected deeply with students. When they see your example of mentoring and hear your own stories—not just stories of other people—and see how it's enriched your life and added impact to your messages, they are more likely to respond to your leadership. Their loyalty will grow. Their satisfaction in serving on the team will likely increase because they sense they are a part of a group that really "gets it" when it comes to high-integrity, high-impact youth ministry. They may want to mentor a student as well, further multiplying the positive effect of what you're doing. Mentoring can play a major role in turning youth groups into youth ministries.

One high school senior wrote this to his mentor, a youth pastor:

Beyond the fact that you are a friend and a spiritual leader, the number one thing you did that helped me grow as a Christian was giving me ownership in what was going on in the ministry. You gave me responsibility, setting clear expectations about what was to be done, and the level of excellence required.

When you felt I was ready to take on a new type of ministry, you gave it to me (whether or not I thought I was ready). You let me run with it. You were always there in the wings to give direction, but in the end it was my responsibility to perfect and make excellent the ministries you assigned. You included me in your own expectations and goals for yourself. This gave me direction to form my own expectations and to realize the potential you saw in me, and increase the potential I saw in myself.

You treated me as a partner, trusted me like a brother, and talked to me as a friend. You valued my opinions, listened to my suggestions, and pushed me to go beyond my comfort zone (sounds a lot like Paul and Timothy, eh?). Through your mentoring and discipleship, I gained the passion to make Christ beautiful and excellent to the world.

Who wouldn't like to get a letter like this? The words of this student ought to inspire all of us who are in youth ministry to build into a few—even as we work to reach as many students as possible. Frankly, effective youth ministry is not about size; large or small, a ministry led by a mentoring pastor and volunteers will be more powerful and more real for everyone who comes. Both the short-term benefits that are obvious and the kingdom gains that we won't see until heaven should lead us to adopt mentoring as an integral part of our overall ministry strategy, and one that Jesus would want. And when you mentor a student or two, you'll wonder why you didn't make it a part of your weekly rhythm a long time ago.

The battle is on and it's time to equip this generation of young students to fight the fight. You can do this. Take a moment to pray, asking God to remove any fear you may have, and to give you confidence that he's chosen you to be a mentor for a few students. Ask him to reassure you of this truth. Then grab your sword—and come out swinging.

The Real World ...

Is mentoring a spiritual gift?

Nowhere in Scripture does it teach us that mentoring is a spiritual gift. Spiritual gifts can help you be a better mentor, but there is no single gift that makes you a mentor. But God will use all the gifts he has given you, and give you all you need to become a mentor. Remember, God is for you to become a spiritual mentor for his kids. How awesome is that?

What do you say to the students who may get jealous because they are not being mentored?

This is a good problem to have: more students wanting to be mentored than you can handle. Find out what the student is jealous about. Then tell them the truth—let them know that they might not be ready yet, or they don't understand the commitment level, or that it might not be a good fit, or that you need to find a mentor for them. Most of the time, students who object aren't sure what they are jealous of or complaining about. They don't truly understand the commitment required (see chapter 4). Make sure that students know that mentoring is not the only way to get involved. They can *all* participate in small groups and other ministry events, and they can still have a *measure* of personal contact with you or other leaders. (Remember, even if you mentor a few students, you will still be able to talk to and shepherd other students within the ministry).

Most of the time, if students understand you are proud that they want to grow as a Christ-follower, and they know how they can get involved (and that mentoring may happen later when they're ready or when a mentor is available), there should be no problem.

I want to mentor, but I haven't been mentored myself. I am not sure what I should do.

The fact that you are reading this book is already a positive step. Sure, you'll have questions, but many will be resolved as you continue to read, and you can figure out the remaining ones as you go. You might find asking other mentors' opinions to be helpful, and you could even meet with them on occasion. Remember, God will use what he has given you. You just need to be open and willing to be an example of Jesus. Don't let fear keep you from mentoring. You can be an example to a student of what a Christ-follower is. Just remember, students are looking for what is real. *You can do this!* Don't let the lack of a perfect example keep you from being a good enough example to a student.

I'm a youth pastor and our senior pastor is focused on the big group. He wants me to take care of all the students—he is not going to thank me for caring for a few.

First of all, he'd thank you if you were mentoring *his* kids! (Okay, we're being a little sarcastic now!) Remember, mentoring does not mean you should stop doing your job as the leader to all the youth, or start making excuses for not wanting to reach more students. But mentoring is the right thing to do, no matter what else is going on. In time, if you work hard, your pastor will see your heart, and we believe he will come around because he'll see students you are mentoring and how their lives are changing. He will notice how volunteers are involved in mentoring, and how excited they are.

Even if he doesn't, the students you mentor will thank you. Your volunteers for whom you're a role model will thank you. We believe God will be pleased. Remember: mentoring *adds* to your overall ministry effectiveness. It really does. And *that* your senior minister will notice. The most important thing, however, is that we believe someday you will get the "thank you" that you really are looking for ... and that is from God when he says "Well done, my faithful child."

As a youth pastor, should I encourage small group leader volunteers or other staff to be mentors?

Absolutely! Get parents, grandparents—anyone who has mentoring potential. This is one of the best things anyone in youth ministry can do. Mentoring will make them better leaders. If they are paid staff, it should be a requirement. Remember, as the point leader, the example should start with you.

I want to mentor a student, but will have to say no to another student who has potential. Frankly, I favor the one over the other. Am I wrong for having a preference?

You need to be sensitive and make sure the student *not* chosen doesn't think you passed them over because you consider another student better. The most important thing is to tell the truth. Let the student know that you believe they'll be better off with a mentor who has a more suitable relational fit. It's important, however, for you to be honest with what you feel. If you start mentoring a student just out of guilt, you may end up hurting the student and yourself. It's hard to explain, but as you pray and ask God's direction, you will know what is right. Some students will connect better with another mentor than with you, and that's okay. Choose wisely and prayerfully. Jesus selected his disciples intentionally out of a large field of candidates. Doubtless *he* had a preference and chose accordingly. We should do the same.

chapter summary

Verse to Remember: Mark 3:14

He appointed twelve—designating them apostles—that they might be with him and that he might send them out to preach.

The guiding strategy for mentoring is what we call the Be-With Factor. It embodies the value of living a lifestyle that includes inviting a student into a close relationship to help that student grow in Christlikeness. We are in a fight for young people's souls and mentoring is one of the best tools in our arsenal—it's how we'll win the war. This was Jesus' strategy with his disciples, allowing them to observe him in a variety of settings so he could model as well as teach. Youth leaders need to lead the way in building into a few students, and mentoring is a great way to keep your passion for ministry strong. It also impacts others around you, who see your example and the impact it is having and consider for themselves the challenge to become a mentor.

chapter 3

A Plan of Action

Proverbs says, "Wisdom calls aloud in the street, she raises her voice in the public squares" (Prov. 1:20). The point of the text is that a kind of wisdom is present in everyday life—"in the street"—and readily available to those who notice. God has diffused a steady stream of truth throughout his universe. We're capable of receiving it if we'll listen—even without having to open a Bible. This "common sense" is from God just as much as the truth he reveals in Scripture.

the grand secret of life

How this relates to mentoring we'll explain in a minute. But as an illustration of the above proverb, a "Grand Secret of Life" is found on every airplane in the world. This message is coded, so you might need a little help interpreting it. Everyone who's ever flown on a commercial airplane has received from On High one of life's most profound lessons.

In the pocket of the seatback in front of you is a safety card. To make it easy to understand, it's illustrated with several drawings of what to do in the event of an emergency. The one picture I want to call your attention to has a woman and a child, and oxygen masks dropping down from the overhead compartment. It looks something like this:

At first, this image looks counter-intuitive. The mother puts on her own mask; only *after* hers is in place does she help her child. *How selfish!* You would think the *child* ought to be the priority—his needs ought to come first. Wouldn't that be the compassionate—even Christ-like—thing to do?

Turns out, it isn't. Without oxygen, the adult is likely to risk both her own *and* her child's well-being. So if you were in that emergency, the correct order of events is to get oxygen for yourself first, then help others. Self-care supports other-care.

That is the Grand Secret of Life.

Lest you think this is self-serving hedonism, note that the most compassionate, selfless person who ever walked the planet lived that way. Jesus practiced input before output. He gave himself to others selflessly, but throughout his ministry he also made sure both he and his disciples had adequate "refueling" experiences, spiritually and recreationally. The Bible also teaches this wisdom "calling aloud to us in the streets" (or from a runway, as it were). "Then, because so many people were coming and going that they did not even have a chance to eat, [Jesus] said to them, 'Come with me by yourselves to a quiet place and get some rest'" (Mark 6:31). So if you want to live like Jesus lived, periodically you'll have to say, "I need to get away to a quiet place and get some rest."

follow the leader — doing as Jesus did

As Christ-followers, we've chosen to heed our Leader's teachings—we do what he said to do. We also mimic his lifestyle—we do the things he did. And once we've decided to become mentors, we let students see this way of life up close. This deliberate choice to let a student see how we flesh out Jesus' teaching is the core experience behind the plan of action mentors use. Mentoring is always about becoming like Jesus, and students learn practical ways to do that by watching how we mimic him.

Much in Jesus' "way of life" is worth copying. Skim through the Gospels some time and notice the "back and forth" nature of his ministry. As we already pointed out, he practiced a sane and sustaining rhythm that enabled him to fulfill a very challenging ministry assignment to the masses, while mentoring his disciples at the same time. Watching his actions closely shows both his humanity and models a profound truth about how ministry and life will go for us. It's true we don't have exactly his same mission—to die for mankind's sins. We are not the Only Begotten Son of God. But on so many other levels, he shows us the way to live—not at all detracting from his unique role as the Way itself.

Consider the following examples. They show rhythms we would do well to pay attention to for our own sake as well as for the students we mentor.

Public	Private
Jesus would engage in ministry activity with vigor.	He made time to rest.
Jesus taught the crowds.	He took time to be with a few.
Jesus ministered to many.	He made sure he had solitude so the Father could minister to him.
Jesus talked to people.	He talked to God.
Jesus gave public messages and people listened to him.	He would ask a question and listen to the person's answer.
Jesus had a public, large-scale outreach ministry.	He ate some meals with small gatherings of seekers.

As we mentor students, we are inviting them to a lifestyle: to follow Christ's way of living in close connection and in daily dependence on our heavenly Father. The way we do that is through what we say, and more importantly, through inviting students to watch how we do it—to get some idea of how following Jesus is done in this day and age. Like the apostle Paul, we say, "Follow my example, as I follow the example of Christ" (1 Cor. 11:1). Did Paul write that because he considered himself a perfect copy of Christ? Of course not! It was both his victories and his struggles that he invited others to learn from. He suggested his *example*—not his "perfection"—be followed.

We mentors are pupils—disciples—of Jesus, first and foremost. We learn about what Jesus taught and how he lived. We imitate those actions and show young students how to do the same in their lives. We believe this model is missing in so many students' lives today. We need to change this reality about youth ministry. It is time for students to hear from real live leaders all over our land, "Follow my example, as I follow the example of Christ."

spiritual practices — no shortcuts

Think of the ways over the years you've learned to keep your relationship with God strong. When you're at your best, what are you doing?

People often use the term "spiritual practices" or "spiritual disciplines" to describe the activities and experiences that Christians use to strengthen their connection to God. Dallas Willard in *Spirit of the Disciplines* has grouped these into two major areas: disciplines of *engagement*, and disciplines of *abstinence*.[1] Among the former are things like prayer, Bible study, worship, and confession; we *engage* someone or some activity. On the other hand, disciplines of abstinence include solitude, silence, fasting, and acts done in secret; in these practices, we *abstain* from legitimate activities or personal contact.

Perhaps you've experimented with some of these. In a mentoring relationship you expose a student to how you practice these in life—which motivates you, by the way, to use more disciplines more often. You show students how you've folded these practices into your daily routine. What may now be something you're beginning to do—or even an established habit—is probably completely untried for a student. Mentoring—"being-with"—allows the student to get close enough to observe firsthand how someone lives the Christian life and engages in these practices.

---

1. Dallas Willard, *Spirit of the Disciplines* (New York: HarperCollins, 1988), 158.

I (Judson) worked with high school students right out of college. After I'd been at my church for a month or so, I picked two young guys I wanted to mentor. One of the things I occasionally did in our times together was to read excerpts from my prayer journal to them. At first, I just wanted them to know what a prayer journal was; I also wanted to help them hear the kinds of things I said to God; and sometimes I wanted them to know I struggled with a lot of things just like they did. Of course, we would pray together often, and they got a sense of how a young man like myself could just talk openly with God in a very natural way. I would also pray with them about how I believed God was going to do great things in our ministry that year. One of the guys finally asked me how I could know the future like that—seeing as I seemed so sure God was going to do such a great work in our midst! I realized they misunderstood, and I had to clarify that my optimism wasn't a prophetic gift; rather, it was simply a godly, faith-filled hope.

watch and learn

A spiritual teacher *explains* things to a student; but a mentor *shows* the student. Jesus taught about prayer publicly, but with his disciples he prayed while they watched, and then he also prayed together *with* them. So as a mentor, you wouldn't just talk about prayer, you would pray with the student and let the student "be-with" you while you pray in various settings. Whereas a teacher might describe how to study the Bible, a mentor does a Bible study with a student; the mentor also reacts biblically, without thinking about it, thus showing that the Word has taken root and is not just an abstract concept. In the same vein, a teacher might provide steps for how to work through conflict, or they might explain biblical principles for dealing with anger; but a mentor takes the instruction further and actually enters conflict, bringing a student along, and modeling how to do so in a healthy way that leads to resolution and reaffirmation of the relationship. On a deeper level, a teacher might explain the reality and pervasiveness of human sin, but a mentor candidly shares his or her own struggles with sin and evidences personal progress over time.

I (Bo) love working out and spend a lot of time in gyms. I remember being in the weight room once and noticing three young guys—probably fifteen or sixteen years old. They were obviously very excited about being able to use all the sophisticated equipment. But they were clueless about proper use, and at times were completely turned around, facing the opposite way the equipment intended. They not only looked silly; they weren't working the muscle group for which the machines were intended. I saw such enthusiasm in these guys, as well as desire. They were motivated. The problem was they didn't have a model—someone demonstrating correct use of the equipment. The tools were sufficient for their purposes, but their lack of understanding and the way they misused the equipment kept them from benefiting as they could have.

It's the same in life. Students are regularly using their bodies and minds in ways that are sometimes just the opposite of what the Divine Designer had in mind. What they need is someone to model a better way to live, consistent with God's desires. They don't need to be preached at. They need to hear someone with flesh say, "Watch me." They need a mentor.

every experience a teaching moment

Mentors capitalize on the reality that it doesn't take a special setting to create a learning setting. The main thing required is for the mentor to take action when events occur to help the student see the available lesson. A wise mentor constantly calls attention to what is happening and asks simple questions that turn mundane moments into mentoring moments.

One youth pastor shared this story of how his uncle mentored him —of all places—in an agricultural setting:

> As a teenager, I spent every summer working on my uncle's sweet-corn farm. While it meant missing out on summer camps and fancy vacations, these summers were very important in my personal growth and development. Spending an afternoon helping my uncle repair a tractor always included conversations about faith and doctrine. And while doing the evening drive to check on fields, I felt full freedom to talk about anything and asked him tons of questions about life, relationships, and God. My faith was reinforced, shaped, and sharpened by these conversations—all in the context of a summer job.

Here are several examples of how you can "be-with" in meaningful ways in a wide variety of settings:

➲ As you drive somewhere together, notice people in cars around you. Ask the student questions, such as, "When people weave in and out of traffic like that, do they really get there much faster? What do you think is at the root of people being in such a hurry? Why do you think someone cutting others off can make people so angry? When you watch me drive, what do you see or learn about me?"

➲ When you stop in a store to buy something, ask questions like these: "What do you think are some of the dangers of using credit instead of cash? What do you think is the reason so many people rack up huge credit card debt? What do you learn about me from watching what I buy and how I interact with people in the store?"

➲ When you hear a song on the radio, ask, "Is that true? Is that really how relationships work, or what love is all about?"

➲ When you see or hear a commercial, challenge the student to think through what is being said. Without getting preachy, comment on how you think advertising cheapens or misrepresents reality, especially relationships and spiritual values.

➲ When you see an obviously attractive member of the opposite sex, don't pretend you don't notice the attraction. Acknowledge the person's good looks—without lusting—and thank God that he appreciates beauty too. Show the student how we can be aware of our desires without succumbing to them. Help them view the opposite sex as a body, mind, and soul, all of which is created by God, precious to him, and to be respected, not lusted after.

➲ When you go to a movie together, reflect on what you saw. "What values did you see promoted in that movie, either directly or subtly? What do you think is more destructive: a movie that shows Christians as hypocrites, or a movie that shows non-Christians who seem to do fine without God? Other than the money, why do you think the people who made that movie went to all that trouble to bring it to the big screen?"

➲ When you get together after being off for the weekend, or when coming back from a vacation, ask, "What do you like to do when you don't have to do anything? When you last wasted time and regretted it afterward, what did you do and why do you suppose you chose that, even though you came to regret it? Here's what I like to do: _____; what does that tell you about me?"

➲ When you go out to eat together, ask, "I've heard obesity is almost epidemic; judging by people around us, do you observe that to be true? Do you think being overweight is just a health issue, or is there a spiritual aspect to it? What eating disorders have you heard of, and do any of your friends struggle with them? Here's my view of how God, diet, and exercise fit together: _____; what do you think?"

➲ When you're any place where you can talk uninterrupted, you could ask, "How would you like to be treated by the opposite sex? What are some rules you generally follow when you're with the opposite sex? From what you've seen me do, describe what you think are my core values when it comes to relating to the opposite sex."

➲ When you invite them over to your house, ask, "What do you think makes a friend's house a place you like to visit, or someplace you dread going to? If Jesus had a house, how do you think he'd keep it and why? What message does the way I keep my house send to visitors?"

what we can give that Jesus couldn't

At the risk of sounding blasphemous, mentors offer students something *over and above* what Jesus provided for his disciples: we can show students our *mistakes*. Jesus called attention to the disciples' foibles or illustrated character flaws through stories, but he had no sins of his own to use as lessons. We have an ample repertoire of things we have done wrong to help those we mentor!

In a paradoxical way, we demonstrate Christ-like humility when we let those we mentor see us as we really are. Jesus never had to admit sin, but he did acknowledge his humanity and lived his life as a humble servant before others. We can be of enormous help to students when they see our humanity and how we process our moral and spiritual ups and downs.

I (Bo) asked several guys I mentored in high school to email me some stories. Coleman, then a high school student, is now a grown man, and responded to my request. I had forgotten all about his story but will share it with you now.

> My mentor, Bo, and a group of us guys used to take trips during the summer. While driving, we stopped at a place to eat. I saw some things going on in the restaurant that upset me. I was kind of making a stink and being a pain in the butt. When we walked outside, Bo had a quick talk with me and told me I was being uptight and making too big a deal about what was going on. It was sort of confrontational—with some anger—and I don't think either of us felt great about it. We got in the van, and I laid down in the back. Bo got in the front seat. About ten minutes into the ride, he reached back, grabbed my leg, and said, "No matter how much we fight, I still love you." It was so like him. And that moment has stuck with me all these years. He made sure things were right, things were cool between us. Today, I am a better father, better mentor, better man, a better leader, a better Christian—because of my mentor, Bo.

You might be saying, "Great story! I wish I'd had someone speak into my life like that. How am I supposed to mentor a student when no one was there for me?" Or maybe you're thinking you shouldn't mentor because you don't have enough confidence. Or maybe you think you've made too many mistakes. You might not believe you have that much to offer. But these feelings of inferiority and insufficiency are common—and often just not true. What you bring is enough if you bring your true self. If you're sincere, if you stay focused on Christ, if you're willing to be real with a student, even the parts of you that aren't finished won't be a problem. *You can do this!* The key is to not be fake, and to stay on a growth track yourself. God can and will use even the "bad" in us as we open ourselves to the Holy Spirit's work and let the student watch our progress.

Perhaps you've thought what your students need is mostly to see "how you do it right." Yes, they need that, but what better way to show a student God's grace than to show it working on our own hearts? Can you see how important it is—how truly life-changing it is—for a young person to see how an adult works through mistakes and missteps? Why do you suppose the Gospels are full of stories of how the disciples bumbled and botched their lessons? *Observing and processing mistakes is one of the main ways we learn.* Of course, if you're committed to posturing and pretending and refusing to admit your weaknesses —and generally don't do a good job facing your issues and dealing with them—that's what you'll pass on to your students. We know that's not in your heart—you aren't that kind of a leader or you wouldn't have read this far. So we invite you to step into what is true about you, both good and bad, and with authentic self-disclosure, let the students you lead see where you are and how you get to the next level. This honesty is what is so needed in the lives of students today.

One veteran youth ministry mentor shares these memories about how God used a tense moment to bring a valuable lesson into focus:

> As a full-time youth worker, I've always chosen one or two young people to "be-with" in my travels. That can include traveling to places where I'm a speaker, running errands around town, and sometimes joining my family on vacation. After doing this for a number of months with a young guy named Chris, he finally turned to me one day and said, "When are you going to start mentoring me?" I asked him what he meant. He said, "When are you going to put me through a discipleship program or curriculum?" I told him that I currently was mentoring him; that at the core, mentoring is to "be-with" each other. I showed him in the Bible where it says, "When they saw the courage of Peter and John and realized that they were unschooled, ordinary men, they were astonished and they took note that these men had *been with* Jesus" (Acts 4:13 TNIV, emphasis added). Mentoring is a way of life, not a curriculum you go through ... it's being with a mature, more advanced person whom you want to be like.
>
> Chris ended up spending so much time with me that people around him began to affectionately poke fun at him because he was like my shadow. I remember one evening when Chris was in our home and my wife and I got into a fairly heated disagreement. Chris thought he should excuse himself and started to leave. As he stood up, both my wife and I told him, "You need to stay and see this part of marriage as well. You need to see the sin-

ful part of your mentor." We worked things out, but he learned a valuable lesson about marriage, how to work through conflict, and how I'm committed to being real with him and helping him see all sides of my life.

We should point out that one of the side benefits of mentoring is that you become more aware of your own progress—or lack of it. That's a good thing. It spurs you on to do better—even as you're honest about ways you're not doing so well. Knowing a young person is watching brings out the best in you. It gives you another solid reason to ensure you work your character muscles, so to speak, which might get flabby if you think no one is looking. Paul wrote, "Train yourself to be godly. For physical training is of some value, but godliness has value for all things, holding promise for both the present life and the life to come" (1 Tim. 4:7–8). Mentoring can actually help you take on an "Olympic mind-set" for your own growth. When you make strides forward and do it authentically (freely admitting it is sometimes hard), you're giving a gift to the student and to yourself.

the real deal — authentic role models

This generation is looking for what is real. They're weary of hype. They're tired of adults who pretend they're better than they really are. They long for role models who are willing to share their life's lessons, and who admit that they haven't learned it all. It's ironic that people in our culture, who used to be role models—athletes, political leaders, teachers, and artists—are backing away from that expectation. Their message seems to be, "Hey, don't look at me; I have no idea what I'm doing—find your hero in someone else." *Who is that someone else our young people can look up to?* Who's willing to say, "I may not be perfect, but I care about this generation and I want to 'be-with' them and offer a real example of someone they can follow"? Jesus calls us to be those kinds of people. He wants others to see his grace at work in us. We're to be the light of the world, a city on a hill. "Let your light shine before men, that they may see your good deeds and praise your Father in heaven" (Matt. 5:16).

The good that God is doing in our lives is supposed to be *visible.* A mentored student is one of the best possible audiences to watch God working in you—just as you are the audience watching God at work in a student.

Take a moment to pray. It's a dangerous prayer, but we invite you to ask God to make you the kind of person willing to let a student watch you—and that the student will see Jesus at work.

The Real World ...

Can you give me a quick rundown on what the requirements are for being a mentor?

It starts with an honest and humble heart (Ps. 51). Obviously, if you're not serious about following Christ or are living in a pattern of sin that you have no desire to be rid of, not only should you not mentor, you should seriously reexamine your relationship as a Christ-follower. That said, if you know you have a sincere and growing relationship with Christ, are willing to learn "on the job," have areas in your life where you know God has worked and are willing to share those, are willing to invest some time and energy to build a relationship, and, of course, if you have a heart for students ... then step on up—you're ready to mentor!

I lead a small group of six students in a Bible study. What's the difference between that and mentoring?

Probably the main thing is the "Be-With" times. If you don't have any influence beyond the group meetings, then you're probably not in enough personal contact to have a mentoring relationship. Also, the commitment to a READY student (see chapter 4) and a clear invitation to mentor (see chapter 6) will give you a better understanding of the difference between mentoring and shepherding.

How does a volunteer like me mentor a student when I only have one hour a week to give to ministry?

You might not be able to mentor yet. But if you can work it out to have the student shadow you during other activities, it may be possible. You *will* have to spend *some* quality time with a student you mentor. But don't get discouraged.

Keep serving with the hour you have, asking God to show you how you might be able to give more Be-With time to a specific student. It certainly wouldn't be fair to say you're going to make a mentoring investment and then not give the student any time. God will show you how and when you need to make this choice. Be patient. The moment will come when you will know it's time to mentor.

There's a student in my youth group who wants me to mentor him, but I don't really have any affinity with him, and I find being with him, well, kind of draining. Yet he seems so willing and enthusiastic. What should I do?

First, encourage the student and let them know how pleased you are that they want to grow in their relationship with Christ. Next, be honest with them. Take the time to explain what it really means to be in a mentoring relationship. Let them know that if they're READY, you're committed to finding the right mentor for them, even though it might not be you. The next chapter details how to find a READY student, but we advise you for now to pay attention to your instincts here, which may also be the Holy Spirit coaching you. You should not feel guilty or obligated; you don't have to mentor everyone who comes your way. A student's willingness is only part of how you choose. In fact, some students you might mentor don't know yet that they should be mentored, and may require some challenging from you to make that decision (as long as they have the other READY qualities). We hope the next chapter will help you make a wise decision that serves you and the student.

chapter summary

Verse to Remember: 1 Corinthians 11:1

Follow my example, as I follow the example of Christ.

We are to follow Jesus' example as well as his teachings. He modeled a way of living and a way of being with God that we need to emulate — and model for students. He had a very public ministry with the masses, and also a very private ministry with a select few. As we copy the spiritual practices of Jesus, we demonstrate these disciplines to the students we mentor, so they can "follow us as we follow Christ" (1 Cor. 11:1). Mentors don't just teach; they say "watch me" and use everyday experiences as learning laboratories. Even personal failures are valuable as the mentor capitalizes on those moments to demonstrate all facets of life with God. Authenticity is key when it comes to the plan of action mentors use.

chapter 4
A READY Student

Without checking in a Bible, how would you explain the method Jesus used to pick his twelve disciples?

Maybe you're like most people who aren't sure what process Jesus used—or if he used a process at all. One commonly held view is that he just walked along, and for reasons unknown, asked various people to become part of his inner circle. When he had twelve, he apparently decided that was enough and stopped asking.

But think about it—if you used that method for hiring at your workplace, what would be the result? Do you think you'd have a world-class staff that could compete and win in your market? Or if you picked players for an athletic team using that methodology, do you think you'd have a championship team and a reputation for being a winning coach?

picking on purpose

Most people see the foolishness of such a chance-driven approach to building a staff or a team. And of course, the Bible concurs: "Like an archer who wounds at random is he who hires a fool or any passer-by" (Prov. 26:10). The image of somebody firing off arrows in random directions captures it perfectly: this approach to assembling a team leaves people wounded. You can't hire any passer-by and expect a profitable company. You can't recruit an untested player to build a winning team. And if you want a student to mentor, you can't just pick anybody.

How did Jesus *really* pick his Twelve? He certainly followed the scriptural advice from Proverbs quoted above: he was deliberate, not random. True, some mystery surrounded the actual qualifications he was looking for, and nowhere in the Gospels does he spell out *exactly* why he picked who he picked. But it's beyond dispute that *he took care*: "One of those days Jesus went out to a mountainside to pray, and spent the night praying to God. When morning came, he called his disciples to him and chose twelve of them, whom he also designated apostles" (Luke 6:12–13). Earlier, Jesus surrounded himself with a larger pool of "followers" who had been in his company for a while. He had a chance to observe these folks and get to know them. Then, after a time of very intense prayer and reflection, he called twelve out of the crowd and made a very specific appointment of them. Only after watching them and interacting with them did he choose. The others in the crowd still followed him and were part of his bigger flock: various places in the Gospels list 70 sent out on assignments and 120 gathered in the upper room after his death. But the Twelve were his handpicked closest associates, and even within that group, he focused on the inner circle of three: Peter, James, and John (Matt. 17:1; Mark 5:37; Mark 14:33; Gal. 2:9).

how to find a king

In the Old Testament, the nation of Israel demanded that God appoint them a king. God eventually granted their request and their first king, Saul, had the superficial qualities we normally associate with success: "[Kish] had a son named Saul, an impressive young man without equal among the Israelites—a head taller than any of the others" (1 Sam. 9:2). Despite these promising externals, his reign was a disaster. Apparently "tall, handsome, and impressive" is not enough to make you a good leader!

The next king chosen was a very different story. When God told the prophet Samuel whom he should anoint, Samuel was surprised at God's choice. Before him stood all the sons of Jesse, and when Samuel saw Eliab, he thought to himself, this one must be God's choice. "But the LORD said to Samuel, 'Do not consider his appearance or his height, for I have rejected him. The LORD does not look at the things man looks at. Man looks at the outward appearance, but the LORD looks at the heart'" (1 Sam. 16:7).

Herein lies an important foundational principle in mentoring. Knowing that you have to choose someone, don't be naïve about whom you select. Based on Jesus' example and God's words to Samuel, at a minimum you need to base your choice on inner qualities, not superficial ones.

Now some mentors might be tempted to think, *The whole point of mentoring someone is to change them, so why should it matter whom I select? I will help them become a better person.* But this overlooks a crucial point: you probably cannot help someone who is missing needed "raw material." *Mentoring shapes what exists;* it doesn't create a mature soul out of nothing. As good a mentor as you might be, you don't have that much power over students. Certain traits need to be "hard-wired" into the person from the beginning. You'll have enough work helping the student grow even when these base characteristics are present. You are almost certain to be frustrated if you fail to make sure at least a few vital qualities exist.

It's also tempting to want to pick the most popular kids or the brightest students to mentor. Certainly it's good to look over those natural leaders for their potential. But popularity and intelligence aren't enough. Look for students who have influence *and* who are willing to have their influence shaped by the mentoring process. It may be that some of their natural leadership over others is misdirected. That doesn't automatically disqualify them; if they are willing to accept your input, it may be a matter of the mentoring process taking their natural leadership abilities and channeling them in the right direction.

We also need to say a word about a student's spiritual age and maturity. You might find a student who is very mature spiritually and think, *That's the kind of student I want to mentor.* Or you may think, *Why mentor her? She already has so much going for her, she probably won't need me.* Conversely, you may be drawn to a new believer, thinking, *I could really help this student get grounded in the faith.* Or, just the opposite: *He is so new in the faith, I'd rather find someone with more maturity*. And of course, spiritual age and physical age have no relation: a senior in high school could be a brand-new Christian or a seventh-grader could have accepted Christ at a very young age and be spiritually grounded. The point in all this is that spiritual age alone doesn't qualify or disqualify a student. You need other criteria to make your selection.

a wild man with heart

One of my (Bo's) earliest memories of Troy was seeing him hanging off the back end of a fire engine with a Mohawk haircut dyed red and gold. The fire engine was part of a small town parade right before an all-star high school football game. Troy was a middle linebacker on the team, and I was one of the coaches.

Troy definitely knew how to get noticed. He waved and screamed like a wild man. People watching the parade were afraid of him, and the officers in the nearby patrol car kept their eyes on him. As I looked at this young kid, I thought, *He definitely isn't afraid to be himself. And that hair! Talk about creativity. I want to get to know this guy.*

During the game that night, I caught sight of Troy on the sidelines, helmet off. He was yelling something at a player on the other team. By this point, he was sweaty from playing hard. The red and gold dye from the Mohawk was running down his face, making him look even scarier. I thought, *Man, does this kid have energy!*

After the game, a couple of players told us how our outside linebacker had been hit so hard during a play that he didn't know where he was. When he got back to the huddle to get ready for the next play, he asked Troy, "What should I do? I can't see, I can't see!" Not wanting to waste a time-out, Troy said, "Don't worry about it. When the ball is snapped, I'll yell, and you just run full-speed into the offensive line." When I heard that story, I knew Troy didn't have much compassion, but at least he had a leadership gift!

At the end of the game, Troy shook hands with every player on the opposing team. He also shook hands with each of the coaches on our team and said, "Thanks for coaching me. I had a great experience." When Troy shook my hand, I told him I wanted to speak to him later and suggested we talk on the bus on the way home. Troy said, "No problem, Coach, I'll see you on the bus."

That conversation marked the beginning of a mentoring relationship I've had with Troy that's now going on almost two decades. We have served together, written books together, traveled, and done ministry around the world together. We've done life together. It all goes back to me spotting a guy I thought had some qualities God might use if he would submit them to God's loving, shaping hand. And Troy's life and ministry are a testimony of what God can do in the life of a young Christian man when he is ready and willing to be mentored.

what to look for

So what are the traits you should look for when picking a student to mentor? To help you select a student, we've identified five core qualities to seek out. Finding these increases the likelihood that you're investing in the right kind of person. To help you remember them, we use the acronym READY.

R — RELIABLE

Luke 16:10 says, "Whoever can be trusted with very little can also be trusted with much" (TNIV). There's a saying that past performance is the best predictor of future behavior. What people have done, they will most likely continue to do. If that is the case, a good place to start in your mentoring search is to look for students who have been reliable. Look at how they have handled responsibilities in the past; that's probably how they'll handle them in the future. Is this person a can-do, finish-what-you-start kind of person? It's true the mentoring process will help them mature, but the student has to have a measure of trustworthiness to begin with.

Think of what you're offering a student: a chance to grow and an opportunity to develop oneself in a variety of areas. You'll be investing a part of your one-and-only life in this person. It is simply not wise to "pour water into a sieve," hoping to fill a person who has porous character. Jesus put it rather bluntly when he said, "Do not throw your pearls to pigs" (Matt. 7:6). The point of that saying is not that swine are such wicked animals; it's more that they can't *appreciate* the inherent beauty and worth of a pearl. So if you've got some pigs, don't be cruel to them—but save your pearls for those who know their value. Love and serve everyone you meet (as Jesus did) but make your best personal investment in students who will receive it, value it, treasure it, and hold it (also as Jesus did). The way you find out if a student will do that is by watching how they handle other responsibility now.

One youth minister shared this experience:

> I had a student in my ministry who got into trouble for stealing a video game from his friend. The parent of the friend called me and asked that I meet with this student. I had a good relationship with the student, and the parent decided that as long as I met with him, he wouldn't press charges. We met for a month, but the student showed no real desire to meet or talk about what he had done. He didn't seem to care about the reasons behind his thievery, nor was he willing to focus on his relationship with God. I did what I could, but frankly, I was wasting my time trying to get through to him in one-on-one meetings. He still comes to our ministry, but he really doesn't desire to grow or work through these important issues. He is definitely *not* ready to be a mentoring candidate.

To use a sports analogy, if you want to help someone become a better pass receiver, he needs to at least have good hands and some ability to catch, or you're wasting your time. A student to be mentored needs to be the kind of person who will take what you provide in the mentoring relationship and hold on to it. If he or she keeps dropping the ball, you should probably train someone else.

E — EXCITED

Students who are excited about the opportunity to be mentored are certainly more likely to benefit from the relationship. Students who are ho-hum should not be chosen. Look for the kind of person who has enthusiasm and energy to grow. Again, mentoring is not so much lighting a fire under a person as it is taking someone who's already in motion and providing guidance and channels for their energy.

In a sense, you as a mentor are laying out rails for a train to run on. If you also have to try to get the engine going, you've doubled your work and decreased the likelihood of a positive outcome. To use another analogy, mentoring is like helping to steer a moving car, not jump-starting a stalled one. Look for students who are internally motivated; maybe they don't always know what to do, but once they've got a plan and some direction, watch out! They will reliably and enthusiastically get the job done. A good way to find out if they have this enthusiasm is to test and see if they are really excited about becoming a fully devoted follower of Christ.

Consider this real-life example:

It has been over ten years now that Jeremy and I have been friends. I was his youth pastor, he was a high school student, but we began to form a friendship when we began a weekly mentoring relationship. I created difficult scenarios in our early meetings to test Jeremy's desire to be mentored. I suggested we meet every Wednesday morning *early* for breakfast at my place. I was single and living with a roommate at the time. Jeremy would sometimes throw rocks at my window to wake me up (it wasn't just a challenge for him to get up early!). We met weekly over coffee and Cheerios to talk about life, girls, the Bible, character, cars, and whatever else came up. Jeremy was excited to meet with me and wanted to learn from me. Not only did this result in a successful mentoring relationship, but we've developed a long-term friendship. Those early morning meetings were a very encouraging part of my weekly schedule.

A — AUTHENTIC

Have you ever met someone who is constantly trying to pretend they are someone they're not? Or someone who is so careless with the truth, you find yourself not trusting what they say? Inauthenticity is a deal breaker when it comes to mentoring. Whatever else a student lacks, it is not a good idea to think you'll be able to "reform" a person who can't be real—or who is a chronic deceiver—through this kind of relationship.

Because mentoring is about deep change, a student who is unwilling to journey to the deep places of his or her life cannot benefit from the relationship—and will frustrate your attempts to help. Good mentoring candidates "show up" with what is there inside them. They may be confused about what they see, and they may not know what to do next, but you shouldn't have to cut through layers of resistance to find out what's going on inside of them. True, we are all more complicated than we know. Yet only a student willing to explore that inner mystery is a suitable candidate: posers need not apply!

D — DARING

Mentoring is an adventure! So the kind of student who will really benefit from this relationship is willing to take some risks. A student who is always "playing it safe" will probably want to play it safe with a mentor, and that will frustrate both of you. In the course of your mentoring relationship, you will throw out some challenges—how will the student respond to those? You will have to speak some hard words from time to time—how will the student deal with that? Also, because you will be calling the student to climb higher and push beyond their current limits, someone committed to comfort and the status quo is not going to welcome that input—thwarting the very reason you are working with them.

Certainly we are not suggesting you limit your mentoring only to students who like to jump out of airplanes! Actually, some people with an outwardly, risk-taker-type temperament are quite averse to being daring in matters of the heart—and some more outwardly timid students are very willing to go boldly forward into uncharted waters of faith and self-discovery. The key is to seek a student who evidences a "hunger and thirst for righteousness," as Jesus put it (Matt. 5:6)—an appetite for personal and spiritual growth that causes a willingness to step out of his or her comfort zone if that's what it takes.

Y—YOUNG

No, the word "young" is not a typo. Of course we know students, by definition, are young. The point here is to look for a youthfulness of spirit—primarily shown in teachability. The freshman who thinks he knows it all is not as "young" as a senior who is humble, willing to learn, and eager to have a mentor point out edges for growth. The type of student who thinks he or she has "seen it all" or who is not willing to have you speak into his or her life will not be a good mentoring candidate. On the other hand, a student who is open, curious, and welcomes your input with a humble spirit is the kind of person who is described in Proverbs 15:31–32: "He who listens to a life-giving rebuke will be at home among the wise. He who ignores discipline despises himself, but whoever heeds correction gains understanding."

One great test for knowing if a student is "young" in this sense is to see how they handle a simple correction. If you sense resistance or they try to make it about you, that's a clue they are not ready to be mentored. On the other hand, if they welcome your input—even if it stings a bit—they are more likely to be the kind of person worth investing in. The Bible actually notes this two-fold reaction to instruction and what it signifies: in Proverbs 9:8–9 we read, "Do not rebuke a mocker or he will hate you; rebuke a wise man and he will love you. Instruct a wise man and he will be wiser still; teach a righteous man and he will add to his learning." Notice the phrase "do not." Like "do not cast your pearls before pigs," it is okay (*commanded*, actually) *not* to try to correct certain kinds of people who won't receive what you're bringing. We could easily read the "do not rebuke ..." to also mean "do not mentor ..." that kind of student; instead, find those who are young in spirit and willing to be shaped and guided.

are you ready for those who are READY?

Do you know a student who has the characteristics mentioned above? God may choose to lead such a student to you out of the blue, but most likely, you will have to go on a search. Like Jesus, you will have to surround yourself with lots of people, watch them in a variety of settings, and then select those to mentor from among the many you know. Make your selection carefully. Make it prayerfully, as Jesus did. Consider this important fact: other than in Gethsemane, prior to his agony on the cross, the Gospels reveal Jesus' most fervent prayers were for *those he would disciple*—and once chosen, he prayed with passion and persistence *over* them. It must have been that important to him. Make it that important to you. Why not take some time right now to ask God to place a READY student in your life? Ask him to give you eyes to see what he sees in a young student, and wisdom and discernment to know how to choose the very one God has prepared just for you to mentor. Be ready yourself—you're about to begin an exciting journey!

The Real World ...

I'm having the hardest time getting past the sense that this whole mentoring thing is a form of playing favorites. How can I pick one student over another without being guilty of favoritism?

What is favoritism, after all? It's treating one person as better or more important than someone else for *superficial reasons* (in James 2:1–4, the example is treating someone with wealth better than less wealthy people because you want their approval). But think about it; if you have children, don't you treat them differently than other kids? Is that favoritism? Of course not, because the criteria are not superficial or selfish:

it's perfectly appropriate to care for your children uniquely because you have a responsibility to do so mandated by the relationship. Likewise, Jesus loved the world but chose the Twelve. That didn't mean others couldn't listen to him or benefit from his ministry. He wasn't playing favorites, but he *was* distinguishing different kinds of relationships for different purposes. And that's what you're doing when you pick a READY student: you're establishing a unique relationship for a purpose, with appropriate (not superficial) criteria. And you still do what you can for every person. "Therefore, as we have opportunity, let us do good to all people, *especially* to those who belong to the family of believers" (Gal. 6:10, emphasis added). Or, as we might paraphrase, "Do good to all the students in your ministry, but *especially* care for those you mentor."

I'm a youth pastor with several volunteers who help in my ministry, and I need to spend time developing them. Won't mentoring a student cut into those relationships?

Not as much as you might think. Bring the student with you to meetings with your volunteers. Let the student see what you do with a volunteer, and let volunteers see what you do with the student. Part of what inspires your volunteers to serve and follow your leadership is how they see you model ministry, and mentoring is a great tool for that—a blessing to them, as well as to the student.

What should I say to parents who are non-Christian or who don't want me to mentor their student?

You must honor the wishes of every parent regarding their child. Certainly you can try to make your case about the benefits that will come from mentoring, but after you've done that, if they still say no, you have to trust in God and move on to choose a different student.

chapter summary

Verse to Remember: 2 Timothy 2:2

And the things you have heard me say in the presence of many witnesses entrust to reliable people who will also be qualified to teach others (TNIV.)

"Who" is as important as "what" when it comes to mentoring. We must carefully choose the students we mentor. Five key qualities to look for can be remembered by the acronym *READY*.

R — Reliable. The student must have demonstrated trustworthiness and handle basic responsibilities well.

E — Excited. The student should be eager to be mentored and be a self-starter.

A — Authentic. The student must be honest and willing to be real.

D — Daring. The student must be willing to grow and be stretched and have an appetite for progress.

Y — Young. The student must be willing to learn, to be teachable and open to receiving feedback and correction.

chapter 5

A Safe Environment

"Watch out for false prophets [or leaders and teachers]. They come to you in sheep's clothing, but inwardly they are ferocious wolves" (Jesus, Matt. 7:15).

Not to sound alarmist, but let's ponder a sobering truth: there are people working with students who will harm them in some way. In fact, there may be a person reading these words who will become a *perpetrator*. Hands holding this book may someday touch a student's body in sinful, destructive ways (or worse, already have).

"Whoa! That's not me!" you exclaim. And thank God if that's true. Yet you need to be aware that someone you know may want to become a mentor as a cover for their intention to seek out vulnerable youth to exploit. The Bible promises what is in the shadows will be brought to light. Dark motives lead to hurtful actions, which will in time display the hidden intentions that gave birth to them.

People who do wrong to students don't just accidentally do so. Many small steps must happen before a big, abusive step occurs. Such plans could be conscious or subconscious, but they are plans nevertheless. We are warned in Scripture to be alert about our inner world, so that we are not "like an ox going to the slaughter, like a deer stepping into a noose ... like a bird darting into a snare, little knowing it will cost [us our] life" (Prov. 7:22–23). Our job as leaders is to interrupt the destructive plans of our sinful nature (and to the extent we can, to help others see and stop theirs) to make sure students have safe people mentoring them in a safe environment. Safety is everybody's concern, not just the youth ministry director's.

good intentions gone bad

Fortunately (despite the need for caution) the overwhelming majority of people who work with students have the best of intentions. But circumstances can come into existence that catch them off guard—and test them. In weak moments, what was unthinkable becomes plausible; what was resisted now seems too hard to oppose. And if a vulnerable or willing person is on the other side of the equation, disaster follows.

We've all heard far too many stories about youth leaders who failed to keep good boundaries, even though it was the farthest thing from their minds when they went into ministry. The tragic results have shipwrecked many a life, and left lasting scars on the church and Christ's reputation in the world.

Paul warned, "Do not plan to do the wrong things your bodies want to do" (Rom. 13:14 WE). Your body may want something it should not have. Or someone else may have such a desire and approach you. Sin only happens when the will cooperates. And because our wills are sometimes weak, we must put in place safeguards so that we (and those around us) who mentor students do so with the utmost integrity.

plain talk about safeguards

This chapter is going to be very practical and very specific. We want students to be safe, and we want those who work with them to be above reproach—even to the point of protecting themselves *from themselves*. Paul taught Titus to "Encourage the young men to be self-controlled. In everything set them an example by doing what is good. In your teaching show integrity, seriousness and soundness of speech that cannot be condemned" (Titus 2:6–8). Similarly, Paul wrote to young Timothy, "Keep a firm grasp on both your character and your teaching. Don't be diverted" (1 Tim. 4:16 MSG). You'll need to watch over yourself diligently and help other mentors around you do the same.

Experience has taught us some basic guidelines for keeping the mentoring relationship safe. Fortunately, a biblically informed common sense will most often guide you to do the right thing if you pay attention to the warnings it gives.

as you begin

Before you actually meet with a student, notify your supervisor of your mentoring intent. If you are on a church staff, it would be the person you report to; if you are a volunteer, it would be the staff person supervising your volunteer work. Discuss the kinds of things you'll be doing with the student and the anticipated frequency of meetings. Ask if your supervisor has any concerns or advice. Also give that person the actual name(s) of the student(s) you intend to mentor and keep in touch with your supervisor as the mentoring relationship develops.

Men need to mentor young men and women need to mentor young women. Exceptions might be made if you are mentoring two or three students who will always be with you in a group. In that case, one of them could be of the opposite sex, but generally this should not be done. Unfortunately, in this day of increasing same-sex clergy abuse, even this standard is not enough to completely protect students. If you or someone in your ministry has a history of same-sex attraction, it is probably best not to be a one-on-one mentor. We need to point out that same-sex attraction is not inherently a more "dangerous" temptation than heterosexual attraction, but both must be rigidly bound so no inappropriate actions occur. If you experience attraction to a student, same-sex or otherwise, it is out of the question to mentor that student; there are plenty of other areas to serve in without setting yourself up for a fall and wounding a student for life.

Be sure you also discuss your mentoring intent with the student's parents. They need to know what you'll be doing with their child, the anticipated frequency of your meetings, the kinds of boundaries you'll be putting in place, the fact that your supervisor is supportive and informed, and any other relevant information. Be aware that parents may respond in a variety of ways. Most will probably be thrilled that you want to build into their child, and will do all they can to fully cooperate with and support your efforts. Some may be baffled that you are taking time with their child; they've never seen anyone make this kind of investment in another unrelated-by-blood person. Still others may be suspicious of your motives. And you may encounter some who simply don't want you to single out their child in this way and refuse to allow it. Whatever the parents' reaction, be sure to let them know you are in complete submission to their wishes for their son or daughter and will be involved only to the extent they allow.

troy and trevor's mom

It was another beautiful day in sunny California. When I (Bo) pulled up in front of the apartment, I was a little nervous. Today I was going to meet Karen. Karen was a single parent and the mother of two brothers I was starting to mentor, Troy and Trevor. I had spoken with Karen on the phone several times before, letting her know about me and about details concerning what her boys and I were doing. I had sensed her appreciation and overall trust as we talked on the phone, but this was the first time we met face-to-face. It was important that Karen knew my heart; I also wanted her to be completely at ease and assured of my intentions as I worked with her sons.

When I knocked on the door, Trevor yelled out, "C'mon in, Bo!" Stepping into the house, I immediately felt at ease. I sensed from the surroundings that Karen had a knack for hospitality. It just felt good to be in her home, and her creativity was evident everywhere I looked. I smiled as I realized where Troy got some of his creativity.

Karen offered me a cup of coffee—chocolate mocha. We sat down at the kitchen table as the guys got ready to go work out with me at the gym. Karen already knew I was a teacher and a coach, and that I spent time with her boys as a part of the youth ministry I led. She asked me questions about my personal life—about my wife and my children. I was happy to share freely, because it was important to me that Karen knew I wasn't some "weirdo," but a father who loved his family and God, and was devoted to the ministry God had called him to. I wanted her to know I was there to support her parenting responsibilities and to help her boys in their relationships with God. When Karen offered to pray for me and my family, I knew that this was going to develop into a good friendship.

As we talked, the guys yelled out questions every once in a while trying to find some lost item. Karen answered calmly, like all moms who are seemingly omniscient about where things were last seen in the house. I paid attention, noticing how the guys treated their mom, knowing I would want to have a conversation about respecting and honoring parents. I also sensed lessons for me as a new dad watching how Karen parented her boys.

It didn't take long for us to find ourselves laughing about the guys, about their differences in some areas, their similarities in others, and how they were always forgetting or losing something. When Trevor and Troy were finally ready to go to the gym, I hadn't yet finished my coffee. Karen said, "Take it with you — don't worry about it." As I got up to leave, I asked about the Christian music I'd heard playing quietly in the background. She told me the name of the artist and then gave me the CD to listen to. I could see where Trevor got his generous spirit.

I was reminded of some very important truths when I left the house that day: how much this woman loved her sons, what a privilege it was to mentor them, how she trusted me with her boys' lives, and how important it was that I had her support. I was also surprised by how much it meant to me that she was praying for me even as I prayed for her. It felt good to know we had a kind of partnership; and I left her house many times with a partially drunk cup of coffee in hand, feeling like I'd been in the presence of a good friend.

Although years and miles now separate us, I know I could walk into her house, sit down over a cup of mocha java, and share memories I have of her two crazy boys — now grown men with families of their own. This entire family has become a part of my family. Through this mentoring relationship, I have received much more than I have given.

the parent connection

Knowing how important parental support can be, one wise youth pastor we know sometimes meets with the parents of students who are mentored by other volunteers in his ministry — not just the ones he personally mentors. He wrote:

> One thing our ministry does is help the parents know their kids are safe. While talking to a parent for the first time about our ministry, I was asked, "Who will be mentoring my son and what kind of things will they be doing?" I responded, "Would you like to view the file we've compiled on your son's mentor?" She said yes. I showed her a profile we put together on every mentor: it contains personal information, marital status,

background information, and a criminal history check. After showing her our safety procedures and giving her a tour of our facility, she had a smile on her face from ear to ear. She said, "I feel completely safe and comfortable about my son being here and working with this man. Thank you for doing this for him."

In addition to your initial conversation with the student's parents, it's a good idea to give them periodic feedback once every two to three months as a sort of progress report. Let them know what you're doing and what changes or problems you see in their child. Ask them for their perspective on how it's going — you'll get some great insights from behavior they see happening at home. One thing that's tricky is knowing how much specific feedback to give the parents, because you're trying to keep confidentiality with the student, while at the same time respecting the fact that the student is a minor and the parents have final legal authority. As a rule, it's best to share less detail rather than more. Describe general trends but try to avoid sharing specific things that might embarrass the student.

Two exceptions to this rule exist. First, if the student displays tendencies to harm oneself or others, you must immediately inform the parents and your supervisor. The other exception to the above rule about feedback to the parents is if you should hear about something *they* are doing that is illegal or is bringing harm to someone. For example, a student you are mentoring might confide in you that her father is molesting her younger sister. Report such abuse immediately to your supervisor and to the authorities, who will conduct an investigation. On the other hand, a student may confide in you that he suspects his mom is having an affair, and his dad doesn't know about it. Without divulging who is involved, meet with your supervisor or pastor to discuss the best course of action. In that case, while the action is wrong and harmful, it is not something you *must* report. It ought to be dealt with sensitively, wisely, and with help from other trusted counselors. Don't make any of these tough judgment calls alone: "Listen to advice and accept instruction, and in the end you will be wise" (Prov. 19:20).

meeting places

Because the heart of the Be-With model is for the student to connect with you in a variety of settings, you may misunderstand an important mentoring guideline: *you and the student should not be alone in a non-public place.* You certainly need times together and you certainly will have to have meaningful conversations that are *private*, but you must not be *secluded*.

For example, on a nice day you could take a walk in the park. You are "alone" in the sense that nobody will interrupt you or listen in on private conversations, but there will be—and ought to be—people within eyeshot at all times. A student could be in your home playing video games or doing a project with you, but only when a family member or another student you are mentoring is there.

One gray area is driving somewhere alone in the car; it is best to keep those times to a minimum, though probably not necessary to forbid them altogether. Again, you and your supervisor should have this spelled out so there is no misunderstanding.

stop, look, listen

Here's a simple way to keep all this clear: STOP, LOOK, and LISTEN. When parents teach their little kids to cross the street, they often use those three words as a way to remember how to do so safely: first, come to a complete *stop*; then, *look* both ways for cars; and finally, *listen* for the sound of what they might not see. Only after that has been done should they step out into the street.

By analogy, when you are in a mentoring setting:

Stop. Before any meeting or Be-With activity, stop to ask yourself, *Is this a wise thing to do with a student?* Consider the situation from a variety of angles. Does your supervisor know where you are? Do the student's parents know where you are? How would what you are doing look to them or to your spouse (if you are married)? Is anything going on that you would be embarrassed to have videotaped and projected onto a big screen at your home church?

Look. Look around you; do you see others? You need to be seen at all times. Meet in public places even if just the two of you are talking alone. Don't go anyplace where there aren't others in the vicinity. This protects the student, and also protects you from false allegations of wrongdoing.

Listen. Check in with your "gut" and with what the Holy Spirit might be saying in your spirit. What is God telling you about what is happening in the moment? Also, as you listen to what the student is saying or as you observe the student's behavior, is there any warning sign—any clue that you might be getting in over your head and that it's time to bring in additional help? Listen on a variety of levels—to the student, to yourself, to your heavenly Father—so you can do what is best for the student and maintain safety.

students' boundaries with us

Not only do we keep students safe by making sure we have appropriate boundaries with them, we need to help students have good boundaries with us. That means helping the student have realistic expectations of you.

It's common for the early phase of a mentoring relationship to be characterized by helping the student learn to trust you. As you spend more and more Be-With time, the student will gradually come to see you as safe and trustworthy, which is as it should be.

But then a curious thing can happen. For some students, you will start to seem "bigger than life" and the student could put you up on a pedestal. They may look at you as a surrogate parent, a deliverer, someone who has come to rescue them and solve all their problems. They may ask for your advice and actually come to depend on it so much they hardly even keep their own counsel. In their immaturity, they lean on you too much. And while this is understandable, and to some extent a normal phase of the mentoring experience, you must keep helping the student see the realistic limits of your relationship. You cannot be available 24/7. You don't always give the right answer. You're not a free therapist. You may not be able or willing to help in a certain situation.

When disappointment hits, the student may overreact and put pressure on you. He or she may get passive-aggressive and close you out. The best way to avoid this reaction is to keep gently letting the student know all along what your limits are, to keep "right-sizing" the relationship. And should an overreaction occur, you should not overreact. Take it in stride, and keep building the student's trust while you help them see that no one in their life is ever going to be perfect—nor should they put such expectations on your relationship.

One mentor admitted to the difficulty of setting these boundaries, and yet affirmed the need to do so:

Spending time together is such an important ingredient for mentoring relationships, and yet I also believe it's important to keep time with my family a priority. That means I'm not always available to hang out with students whenever they want. Saying "no" occasionally to going out to eat, playing cards, video game tournaments, watching a movie, etc. is not easy. But my students know that I am committed to investing myself in them — and that investment comes *after* meeting my family's needs. While they are occasionally disappointed when we can't hang out as much as they want, they are seeing an example of what it means to be a good husband and father. I think it will help them for their future families and possibly even improve their attitude toward their families now.

It is common for young people to see situations in black-and-white, all-or-nothing terms. This is especially true in their relational world, where friendships and romantic relationships tend to travel on a roller-coaster of emotions. It takes maturity for them to see that although they came to trust you and now you've let them down in some way, the truth is you are a good friend and are worthy of their trust — though not in the absolute way they naïvely fell into. Navigating this troublesome relational channel is all part of the process, and it's up to you to expect it, be wise about it, and do all you can to prepare for it. Don't get dragged down by the student's relational immaturity.

Jesus' relational boundaries

We know that Jesus was very loving to all people — he was love incarnate. Yet he accepted limits in his relationships and even set boundaries that sometimes disappointed people: he didn't always do what others expected him to do, and at times he turned down their requests.

How is it possible to love people and disappoint them at the same time? The only way to do that is to have a sense that you are doing all God wants you to do even if you're not doing what they want. By pleasing God and loving him first and foremost, you are free to love others within life's limits. There will be times you have to set those limits — even when opposed — but with God's help, you can do that and be free from guilt that somehow you're not doing what is right.

We must listen to God in order to know where those limits are, and ultimately be people who trust God for perfect love, knowing that no human being will ever give it in a measure that meets our deepest needs. When we set out to care for people, it is easy to think that loving them will give us something in return. God has wired us so that those benefits usually occur. But we cannot mentor a student with the idea that somehow our loving them will satisfy our need for love in return, any more than Jesus could have loved sinful people hoping they would love him back and make him feel like it was all worth it. Love has to be a "give-away" without strings attached. Paradoxically, by modeling for a student this kind of love, we often *do* experience a very satisfying return. But when we seek that return for its own sake, it probably won't happen, and a student may actually feel used because they sense our need for their response. It also prevents us from reproaching students because we fear they won't "like us." We need to have a solid sense of spiritual authority and courage to stand our ground when appropriate.

Jesus was able to minister to so many so well because he didn't "need" people. His relationship with his heavenly Father was so secure and satisfying that he could give himself to sinful people—who would disappoint him—knowing that loving them was the right thing even when it wasn't the easy thing.

Notice the following passage from the gospel of John. It's a curious verse, easy to misunderstand: "But Jesus would not entrust himself to them, for he knew all men. He did not need man's testimony about man, for he knew what was in a man" (John 2:24–25). The Contemporary English Version puts it this way: "But Jesus knew what was in their hearts, and he would not let them have power over him. No one had to tell him what people were like. He already knew."

Jesus was able to love people because he was under no illusion that they would be able to meet his deepest relational needs. He knew he had to trust his heavenly Father for that kind of love. That freed him up to be gracious and loving to everybody else—including good people who would disappoint him or bad people who would betray him. He could also love his enemies. Love for others could be a gift, because he was secure in his Father's love.

Likewise, we are to love those we mentor and show them that they must have as their first and foremost relationship, a connection with their heavenly Father, not with us (or their spouse, their parents, or anyone else; see Matt. 10:37). We *rely on* and *trust in* our God ... then we *love* people. It gets really messy when we turn that around and rely on or overly trust flawed human beings.

safety summary

A safe environment for mentoring requires practical steps on the outside and fortifications on the inside. Students will be well-served by mentors who follow simple, common-sense rules for the Be-With times; who *stop*, *look*, and *listen* whenever they are together; and who pay careful attention to setting good boundaries internally as well as externally.

Consider using the following checklist to remind yourself of how to maintain a safe environment. Likewise, be sure any other mentors you work with keep these guidelines in mind at all times. Remember, we need to work together and not let the enemy disqualify any of us. As you go through the checklist below, pray and ask God to protect you and all those who are mentoring. Let him hear us as one heart, asking for his protection as we reach and lead this generation for Christ.

The Safe Mentor Checklist
Stop, Look, and Listen

☐ Does this activity or conversation pass the common sense test?

☐ How would I feel if what I am doing were projected onto a large screen for my whole church to see?

☐ Does the person who supervises me know where I am and what I'm doing?

☐ How would a loving parent feel about what I am doing with their child?

☐ Am I in eyeshot of someone other than the student?

☐ Am I feeling attraction or any other emotion that is inappropriate?

☐ What do I sense God saying about this conversation or activity?

☐ Is the student presenting an issue for which I need outside help?

The Real World ...

Sounds pretty scary. Lots of bad people out there. How can I be sure one of them isn't in the group I'm with?

You can't be *sure*, so you must be *cautious*. Have a plan. If you're not the point leader, talk to that person about getting a plan everybody abides by. Screen each volunteer and have a written child protection policy that every parent receives. And while we have to issue this warning, experience tells us the vast majority of folks mean well and will do well. With a good plan in place, you won't have to worry.

I have a hard time setting relational boundaries and might get overcommitted or feel guilty about what I'm not doing. Should I mentor at all?

You certainly need to be careful. If you know that you struggle with boundaries, the first step is for you to get some help. Maybe consider getting some Christian counseling. On the other hand, this could be a great exercise in developing better boundaries. Find some people to hold you accountable, to walk with you and give you wise counsel, and do not go it alone. The key is to protect the student and you, and to provide a great example in the mentoring relationship. We all have stuff we're working on, and if we have to wait until we're perfect to do ministry, no one will be a mentor. Remember, you can do this. Take the first step. Spend some time in prayer and God will direct you from there. The fact that you are aware of your weaknesses is already a step in the right direction.

I don't want the hassle of having to set boundaries for a student who gets the wrong idea. The whole idea of having to work so hard to make sure I'm not misunderstood seems so bothersome. I'll just stick to other activities and take a pass on mentoring.

Slow down ... not so fast! We all know ministry is hard work, and there are obviously some risks in all youth ministry. The presence of difficulties should not be the measure of whether or not to do something. God may be calling you to take a step of faith. This may be exactly what he wants you to do. Please reconsider; the benefits far outweigh the cost—for both you and the student you mentor. Talk to someone who is already in a mentoring relationship; it may help you to get a better perspective. We are all needed to make a difference in this generation—that includes you!

chapter summary

Verse to Remember: Proverbs 19:20

Listen to advice and accept instruction, and in the end you will be wise.

Students need safe people to be their mentors. Even the best of us need to follow some commonsense guidelines to make sure we and the students we mentor have that safety. Mentors should have open communication with a student's parents so they are informed of both our intentions and activities. The simple rule "Stop, Look, and Listen" can help keep the relationship safe whenever you're together:

Stop to ask if this is a wise activity,
Look to make sure someone else is around, and
Listen to your gut and to the Holy Spirit for warnings about what you're doing.

We also need to set realistic boundaries with the students so they don't expect attention or time from us that we cannot or should not give. And we should personally be checking in with other trusted mentors to make sure we are not acting in any inappropriate ways.

chapter 6

A Clear Invitation

On the day Jesus called Simon and his brother Andrew to follow him, they were in the middle of their work, casting a net into the water. Jesus stepped into what for them was a common situation, and in a compelling way challenged them to follow him on an extraordinary adventure. While they could have had a good life running their family fishing business, Jesus wanted them to "be-with" him—to move beyond earthly ambitions and consider a kingdom vision. In the process, Jesus would make them into "fishers of men" (Matt. 4:19). His invitation was creative, but more importantly, it was *clear*. They knew that Jesus was inviting them to something significant, a relationship that would change their lives forever. Admittedly, some mystery surrounded exactly *how* that transformation would happen, but there was no question the methodology would involve the Be-With Factor, and that they would undergo a metamorphosis from fishermen into fishers of men.

deliberately chosen

One thing that makes a marriage bond strong is that each person deliberately chose the other. You cannot choose your parents or your siblings, but when you get married, you say "I do" willingly to another human being. The process of seeking, meeting, and finding out about the person, and then deciding to make the relationship permanent, helps two people stay committed. If you're married, chances are no one forced you into the relationship. You had a wide field to choose from, so to the one you chose, it says much regarding how you feel about the person.

Mentoring is obviously not as permanent or sacred a relationship as marriage, but the power of choice is still a strong and powerful motivator. You as a mentor can choose among many potential students. It is good for both you and the student to start there, with that realization, and to go forward with the base understanding that both of you are *choosing* this relationship for a season. While it's possible for the student to fall prey to unhealthy pride or a sense of favoritism, that's a risk worth taking. This is also an attitude that can be addressed early in the mentoring process. It's good for the student to know you could have selected others but have decided to invite them into the relationship. Likewise, you realize the student could choose to do many other things with their time, but they are willing to make meeting with you a priority. Such a foundation helps you both know this relationship is worth investing in, and when you are tempted to walk away if things get a little rough, you can return to the significance of the commitment you made to each other.

waiting and trusting

We had just finished the worship set with a time of prayer and reflection. As I (Bo) looked around at the sixty high school students gathered that evening, I felt a true sense of God's presence. Brad, an eighteen-year-old kid who had only been leading worship for a short time, had done a wonderful job leading us into the presence of God.

After worship, Brad laid down his guitar and began sharing what God was doing in his life. As I watched him open the Bible and teach, he looked confident — yet humble.

I had been mentoring Brad for about a year and a half. I couldn't help but be proud of him. He'd been through several trials, and I saw him persevere and patiently wait on God. Now God was using his gifts to speak to his peers and to help others find God's love.

This was a very different picture of Brad than the one I'd seen when I first met him three years earlier. I was a football coach at the high school he attended. I didn't know Brad very well, but he knew me from the Bible study and youth ministry I led. I was surprised one day when I came to practice and saw Brad standing there, waiting to talk to me.

He seemed nervous, and he beat around the bush a little before he finally said, "Bo, would you be willing to mentor me?" I could tell it took a lot of courage for him to ask. As I looked into his eyes, I saw a mixture of fear and hope. He seemed both afraid I might say yes, and at the same time, guarded against disappointment if I said no.

I put my hand on his shoulder and said, "Brad, thanks for asking me to be a part of your life. It's exciting to see your desire to grow in Christ. But we need to back up a little and work through this. Why don't you meet me after practice and we'll talk about what's involved in a mentoring relationship."

When I met with Brad after practice, I asked about where he was in his life, what he really wanted to do, and what steps he wanted to take in his relationship with God. I listened to his story and could tell this was a kid who really wanted to grow. But he wasn't ready yet for a mentoring relationship. I explained to Brad the commitment it took for someone to be mentored, and honestly told him I didn't think he was quite ready. But I made sure this young guy heard me say I was proud of him and believed in him. And in the meantime, I challenged him to take a few steps on his own.

I prayed with Brad and once again reminded him that I was so glad to see his heart grow. As the conversation ended and Brad walked away, I prayed, "God, protect him." I also wondered if Brad would take up the challenge I gave him to attend Bible study.

Brad did show up the very next week. I told him how good it was for him to be there, welcomed him, and made sure he felt a part of the group. That evening I mentioned that we were looking for someone to lead worship. Brad walked up to me afterward and said he was interested. When I asked if he played the guitar, he said no. But he also said he'd be willing to learn. I didn't want to discourage him and I saw how much he wanted to be involved, so I said, "Brad, if you can get a guitar and learn a few basic chords and some of the songs, let me know and we'll talk." My purpose with Brad was to lay out challenges and wait to see what he would do.

Fast forward three years: as Brad closed the evening in prayer, I was so thankful to God for how he is able to develop young men and women, use their gifts, build confidence, and put them in positions to lead. Even though I had to tell Brad to wait when he first approached me, God can do amazing things when we are willing to trust him, make our mentoring selections carefully, and always speak the truth in love.

the first meeting

Before you make a formal invitation, you need to identify "READY" students (see chapter 4) and choose among those. And you need to know each student's "story": their background, their family situation, and how long they've been a Christian *before* you have this first meeting. After you have prayerfully made your choice and sense God's confirmation, the next step is to arrange a meeting with the student to present your offer of mentoring and to lay out what would be involved if the student agrees. Here's a step-by-step outline you can use (or adapt) for that first meeting. This is a very important meeting; take your time and don't rush. Pick a quiet, public place (for example, a coffee shop or café) and plan for about an hour. Remember to have fun and watch God work!

Explain your intentions.

Tell the student about how you came to see mentoring as an important part of your ministry. Explain that your hope is that each student you mentor will become more like Christ and more connected to him. Explain that the heart of mentoring is Be-With times, and that your intention is to connect with the student in meaningful ways in real-life settings. Also point out that mentoring is not necessarily going to make the two of you "best friends"; rather, the goal is to grow in character and to have a stronger walk with God.

Share why you chose the student.

This part of the discussion is an important moment of affirmation. Tell the student exactly what you've seen in them that makes you want to build into their life. Let them know the specific "READY" qualities you observe, as well as other feedback that would help them understand your view of them. Look the student in the eye and give messages like, "I see this in you ... I believe in you ... you can do this ... God is at work in your life and here's how I see it."

Let the student know you've prayed about the matter and sense God's confirmation.

Explain the commitment.

You might be tempted to "soft-sell" this part of the agreement, but don't. The total time commitment averages approximately two hours per week: one meeting for a formal study/discussion (about two hours every other week), and then time together doing things that are part of everyday life (again, about two hours every other week). In addition, there will be some assignments you make as the year unfolds; these may involve outside study and reading, serving experiences, and "stretches" that you deem appropriate at the time (probably not more than another hour a week on occasion). Phone calls and emails may also take some time (experience will show you how much you tend to do those things as a mentor). Your plan may vary from this rough outline, but whatever you decide on, be clear about your expectations. Let the student know both you and they will pay a price to make this relationship happen, but that you believe it is worth it. Keep in mind you're making an investment too, and you do not want to build into someone who is likely to bail at some point in the future. Let the student know it may not be easy; that it's possible at some point they may want to quit, but if they say yes, then everyone is in agreement to see it to the finish (generally a nine-to-twelve-month commitment—one school year—with an option to do a second year if both of you agree it's a good idea). It will take perseverance, and the student will need to be willing to go further spiritually and relationally than ever before. Time together will be a priority, meaning some other good, perfectly legitimate activities will have to be sacrificed. Just as Jesus didn't mention anything about convenience or ease in his call to discipleship (Luke 9:23–24), neither should you. Of course it will be worth it (Mark 10:29–30)—you're calling the student to a higher standard of living, but that's different from saying it will be *easy*.

Discuss their questions and any concerns.

Because you've been doing most of the talking, this is the time to give them space and to listen. (Notice how even as you conduct

this meeting, you're modeling the Be-With philosophy by caring for the student, giving them feedback, and actively listening.)
Whatever is on their mind at this point is a good indication of
things to come. Pay attention to what they ask about and how
open they are. If they don't ask any questions, ask a few of your
own so you are sure they understand what you've been talking
about:

➲ How do you feel about making this commitment?

➲ What do you think will be the benefit to you by doing this?

➲ What do you think you might have to give up to make this
work, and how hard will that sacrifice be?

➲ What difficulties do you anticipate?

➲ How do you think God might want to stretch you in this
relationship?

➲ What do you think your parents will say about the mentoring
relationship?

➲ How do you want to be different by next year?

Make sure they don't respond with a glib, "Sure, whatever, why
not" attitude. A thoughtless response probably means they're not
getting it—or they are the type of person who says yes too easily
and gets over-committed and doesn't finish. Press them to go deeper
as they contemplate what's involved in a mentoring relationship.

Ask for a commitment.

Specify a time limit for the student to pray about the decision
(probably a week or two) at which time they will give you an
answer. Encourage the student to talk to their parents and at least
one other person. Note that in suggesting these steps, you're showing them a good model for decision making based on prayer and
counsel (Prov. 20:18; Ps. 127:1). If the parents don't know you at
all or are interested in more information about you, this would
be a good time to give the student a filled-out "Mentor's Personal
Profile" (see the end of this chapter) and have them share it with
their parents. As we said in the preceding chapter, it's best to have
a personal conversation with the parents at some point, but the

Profile is a good first step in helping them get to know you. Be sensitive to parents who are not believers. Avoid "churchy" lingo and be open to how you might minister to them as well as to their child. Encourage the parents to talk to your supervisor also: the staff person you report to if you're a volunteer, or your boss at church if you're on staff.

Here's a great idea from one youth pastor summing up his ground rules for initiating a mentoring relationship:

> Whenever I start a relationship with a student, I like to be clear about what I'm after. I generally have three rules I want to set as expectations. First, I tell the student what kind of vision I have for them. I make it clear that I see a ton of potential in them and feel led by God to invest in them. I get really specific. Second, I set up some time frames. How consistently will we meet? I also like to tell the student that when either of us has two or three things to discuss, we need to call each other between meetings. If the list gets to four or five items, that means we've waited too long. Lastly, I make it clear that whenever they call, I will make them a priority. I request they do the same. These steps help make the arrangement between us official. It just doesn't work to try to mentor someone who isn't on the same page.

how many students?

We've touched on this before, but as we close this chapter, it's a good idea to know and right-size your capacity for mentoring at this point. If you're a youth ministry volunteer, you'll do well if you have only one student to mentor (in addition to whatever other responsibilities you carry). After you've done this once or twice, you might find your capacity is greater and you could take on another student, but it's probably better to mentor one student well than to end up mentoring three students poorly.

If you are in full-time youth ministry, we urge you to take on two or possibly even three students (though not more). Your ministry capacity ought to be greater than that of individuals on your team. In terms of the feedback you get from the students, it's hard to overstate how beneficial it is to you to have these students in your inner circle, giving you constant access to the real-life ups and downs of being a teenager. These students will also tell you the truth about what's *really* going on in the ministry. Welcome that, and invite them to speak freely. Remember, you don't just give to students; those you mentor help keep you sharp and their experiences help you be a better all-around youth pastor. Plus, by mentoring two or three students, you see more fruit over time—and isn't that why you're in ministry?

The Real World ...

All this interviewing and formal invitation stuff—it's not my style. I just want to hang out with some students and see what God does.

Go ahead, hang out with some students. Certainly good can come of that. But don't call it mentoring, because the *intention* and *invitation* are at the heart of the relationship and are what helps it succeed. In the same way a marriage is made strong by clear boundaries, a good mentoring relationship is made strong by a clear delineation of who's "in" and what "in" means. Jesus *named* his disciples, even though he had other people he associated with (Lazarus, Mary, Martha, etc.). You need to name the students you're mentoring, and they need to know you are their mentor.

You've certainly laid out a lot of points to remember during the interview. What if I forget something when I have my first meeting?

If you have trouble, make some notes and bring them with you. Remember to be real. Take a deep breath, relax. You're going to be fine.

Okay, what about this: what if the student says "no"?

Students get to make their own choice in this matter. People said no to Jesus too, and he let them walk. Perhaps you could press them a little, but you shouldn't have to manipulate this relationship. Saying "no" might actually be a good choice and indicates a level of maturity and honesty that should be applauded. They might be in a season of life where this commitment would overwhelm them. And students can still be involved in ministry, in small groups, in serving, and in all the other things you're doing, and benefit even though they're not being mentored.

If the student does say no, make sure they know you still believe in them and look forward to having them involved in other activities within the youth ministry. Make sure they don't feel you are disappointed or mad, but that you honor their decision.

What if a student asks me to mentor them, but they aren't READY, or I just don't believe I'm the right person for this student?

Be encouraging, even if you say no to them. And be honest. You could ask them what they really want; if they're not a READY student, they may have other needs (to want a friend, to be accepted by a leader, to be seen, etc.). Have them spell out what's behind their request, and help them see they may be looking for something besides mentoring. Affirm that you're glad they have an interest in growing, but explain that their commitment level isn't enough, or that you have other students in mind and don't have the capacity to mentor one more student (or whatever the reason is you don't think they're READY). Encourage them with all the other ways they can grow: for example, being involved in your program, getting in a small group, going on mission trips or to camp, serving in the church, and learning by reading Christian books. The key here is for the student to feel your full support and not rejection. Be gentle and honest.

chapter summary

Verse to Remember: Matthew 4:19

"Come, follow me," Jesus said, "and I will make you fishers of men."

Jesus made a deliberate and careful choice of his disciples and gave them a clear invitation into the relationship. We must do the same with the students we mentor. After finding a READY student (and if you're in full-time ministry, we recommend finding two or three), it's time to meet with the student(s) and lay out the mentoring vision.

1. Explain your intentions.
2. Share why you chose the student.
3. Explain the commitment.
4. Discuss any questions or concerns.
5. Ask for a commitment.

We also encourage you to create a written mentor's profile to share with the student's parents so they are also clear about the invitation you're extending to their son or daughter.

Mentor's Personal Profile

Mentoring is a great privilege and responsibility. Because I want to foster open communication, here's a little background on me for your information.

Mentor's Name:

Address:

Phone numbers:

Email:

Age:

Marital and Family Status:

My supervisor, to contact if you have questions about me or what I'm doing:

Here's a little about my spiritual journey so far:

Some of the youth ministry experiences I've had are:

Here's why I want to become a mentor:

I believe I will be a good mentor because:
The kinds of activities we'll be doing while mentoring are:
I have the following expectations from your son/daughter:
Frequency of our meetings: (example: Once a week for 1 ½ hours)
Duration of our mentoring experience: (example: Nine months with a possible second season)
Ways to foster a good mentoring relationship: (examples: Keep commitments, be real and honest in conversation, be willing to be challenged, desire to be closer to Christ)

chapter 7

A Plan for Meetings

So you've made your invitation to a student to be their mentor, talked to the parents, the student has prayed about it ... and the decision is "yes." That means you're now officially a mentor. Congratulations!

Then panic sets in. "Oh no," you exclaim to yourself. "Now I actually have to *do* something with the student!"

Don't worry, we've got two more chapters to make everything crystal clear!

Jesus starts his mentoring

Remember how in the earliest stages of Jesus' public ministry, he spent time with various people, and then out of that crowd, picked the Twelve? It's instructive to note that after that appointment, we see Jesus balancing two competing priorities: first, he wanted the disciples to be with him as he conducted his public ministry, but second, he wanted to be alone with the disciples in private meetings.

For example, right after Jesus returned from the mountainside where he first named the Twelve, he entered a house and had a private meal with the disciples (Mark 3:13–35). At least, they *started* to have the meal alone—but then a crowd gathered and they ended up having a more public ministry session. Right on the heels of that, Jesus taught the famous parable of the sower to a large crowd by the lake, but that gathering dispersed and is contrasted by a private tutoring session where the confused disciples received additional instruction on the meaning of the parable (Mark 4:1–20). Clearly, Jesus had meetings apart from the crowds, where he taught his disciples more in-depth. The gospel writer, Mark, explains this back-and-forth rhythm of Jesus' teaching in these words: "With many stories like these, [Jesus] presented his message to [the crowds], fitting the stories to their experience and maturity. He was never without a story when he spoke. When he was alone with his disciples, he went over everything, sorting out the tangles, untying the knots" (Mark 4:33–34 MSG).

Your meetings with students are like those private teaching sessions Jesus had with his disciples, where you "sort out the tangles and untie the knots." Some of those meetings will be a formal study and discussion; some of those times will be just hanging out and talking about whatever comes up. You be the judge of how best to use the times when you two are together. Our suggestion is to start with one meeting each week, alternating between a formal Bible study one week and a more informal Be-With time the following week.

Jesus' kind of Bible study

For the rest of this chapter, we want to unpack what those formal meeting times will look like. If you are mentoring more than one student, you can hold these meetings with all of the students at once—the addition of the others can be a plus for discussion purposes. The other Be-With times that are not a study should probably be one-on-one or one-on-two.

Most youth workers are familiar with Bible study–type small group gatherings. At their most basic, these meetings consist of prayer and discussion on a passage of Scripture. While those elements are also the foundation of mentoring meetings, we want to provide more detail and clarify the philosophy behind using the Bible effectively in the mentoring context.

We really do believe that truth from God's Word is a catalyst for the spiritual change that we desire to see happening in students' lives. If you think you can feed a human soul at its deepest level by just sharing your own wisdom—however good that might be—we urge you to submit to what Jesus said (reaffirming an Old Testament claim): "Man does not live on bread alone, but on every word that comes from the mouth of God" (Matt. 4:4). Truth from God's Word must nourish a student's famished life. It must illuminate the darkness and foolishness that the world around us calls "normal."

That said, it is not simply a matter of pressing biblical principles into the wet cement of their young minds—as if crammed content will produce Christ-like character. Students need to grasp, hold fast to, and treasure God's truth—not just parrot it back. In our experience, one of the most glaring errors among some youth ministries is the notion that if students can recite Scripture truths or "say the right answer" when quizzed, they are somehow sufficiently formed by that truth. Worse, some leaders think that if their messages preach those truths, that *alone* guarantees they've done all they're supposed to do—as if saying the right thing (regardless of what the listeners hear) is adequate. But statistics show otherwise: an alarming number of churched students go away to college and begin to build their adult lives unyielded to God and his ways—though they appeared to heed God's truth while in high school. One pollster found 42 percent of high school seniors stop attending church by age twenty-five, and by age twenty-nine, 58 percent are no longer involved.[1]

As an example of this trend, here's what one nineteen-year-old wrote about his experience his first year after high school:

I was raised in the church and was viewed as one of the committed kids in my youth group. I really thought I had my faith figured out. My intentions were to get involved in a church when I went away to college. But when I got there, everything changed. I was surprised at how little I knew and how unsure I was about my faith—I didn't even know what I really believed. I actually started to doubt God and wondered if I even needed him. I never thought I would get to the place where I would question God. But I am now. I wish that I had had someone in my life in high school who would have taught me about real life and how to walk with God. I just feel so unprepared.

1. Barna Research Group, Ltd., "Twentysomethings Struggle to Find Their Place in Christian Churches," September 24, 2003 *Barna Update, www.barna.org*.

We believe that part of the antidote to this problem is to be sure that our teaching in large gatherings, small group meetings, and even one-on-one times grapples with truth and shows real-life scenarios where principles from God's Word make sense and actually work. We believe it's better to take one powerful truth and hammer it home, repeat it, come at it from a variety of angles, and show the inferiority of all other alternatives, than to try to cover massive amounts of teaching at a surface level and leave students unconvinced and uncommitted to any core life-practice or principle. And the best antidote of all: we long for students to have the opportunity to see up close how a real-live adult lives in daily connection with God. Friends, *that's mentoring*!

say that again, with a question

As you read the Gospels, you can't miss how Jesus stresses several themes over and over in his teaching, telling multiple stories with essentially the same point (for example, Luke 15 where the lost sheep, lost coin, and lost son all point to a similar lesson that "lost people matter to God"). He wanted his disciples to "get it," so he taught publicly and privately; he repeated himself and engaged them in discussion rather than only lecturing. He made them think not just by what he said, but by what he asked *them* to say. He knew those he sought to minister to had to hear *themselves* talk as well as hear him talk; both kinds of hearing were means to evaluate, process, and incorporate God's truth into their lives.

For example, when considering one of the most important issues for the disciples to understand, namely, his true identity, Jesus began with a question, "Who do people say I am?" (Mark 8:27). When they answered by quoting a number of current theories, he asked another question, as if to say, "Okay, that's all very interesting; you've done your job and surveyed popular opinion. But this isn't just an intellectual exercise: following me may cost you. And your eternity hangs in the balance. So who do *you* think I am — what's the answer *you're* willing to stake your soul on?" (see Matt. 16:15). When Simon Peter answered correctly, Jesus affirmed the deep spiritual reality that Peter's answer exposed and how valuable that truth would prove to be to Peter and the entire Christian movement (Matt. 16:17–18).

In another instance, someone asked him, "What must I do to inherit eternal life?" (Luke 10:25). If a student were to ask that question in a typical youth meeting today, he would be barraged with talk-talk-talk, pamphlets, and four-point outlines—and an hour later, would regret having stepped on what was apparently some kind of spiritual land mine packed with verbal shrapnel! Yet Jesus—heaven-sent truth incarnate, the only human with *all* the right answers—responds to this person's question by asking him a question! Isn't that a waste of time for the One who is truth himself to ask a sinful person for his opinion? Here's a paraphrase of what Jesus said: "Great question. Can't think of a more important one, actually. So, I'm wondering ... what do *you* say? How do you answer your own question, given what you know of the Bible?" (Luke 10:26). Jesus could have just given the answer, but he knew *interaction* would be far more effective.

When you meet with your students, select or create material that helps them understand truth in "bite sized" portions, with "super-sized" application in daily life. Make sure they are engaged and that you are asking questions, and that the answers to those questions really matter. Avoid a curriculum that is too theoretical, too "heady," that either has no scriptural mooring or doesn't help students see the meaningful ways Scripture connects to their lives. If you're willing to actively lead using this philosophy, many different materials will suffice. You can pick a published curriculum, adapt one of those as needed, or create your own. We've written a starter series of lessons called *The Be-With Factor Student Guide: Six Questions Students Need to Ask About Life with God* and the appendix of this book serves as a leader's guide for that material.

At Willow Creek, we use a convenient outline, called the Five G's to help our members get the big picture of their spiritual life. The Five G's are: Grace (the foundation of our life with God), Growth (progressing as a Christian), Groups (relationships that optimize life-change), Gifts (God-given abilities used for the common good), and Good Stewardship (the reasonable response to our gracious God). These can form a good outline for study and life review, and several published materials use the Five G's as a foundation (for example, *G-Force: Taking Your Relationship with God to a New Level* by Bo Boshers and the *Pursuing Spiritual Transformation* series [six study guides] by John Ortberg, Laurie Pederson, and Judson Poling).

meetings that matter

In addition to doing some kind of Bible study and discussion, it's a good idea to take some time to pray when you meet. Many students have never had intimate prayer times with an adult, so you are modeling what may be an unfamiliar but powerful aspect of a mature Christ-follower's life with God. These times do not have to be long or drawn out, especially if your student is a new believer. Gradually increase your prayer times as you sense the student is comfortable.

As you pray, students open themselves up to the presence of God. His work in these moments is a powerful, transformative experience. Sometimes prayers won't be answered in the way you hope, but that can become a learning crucible. And surely the answers that *do* come are exciting and faith-building too.

Just as all your conversation together needs to be honest, your prayers need to be honest as well. If the student senses that you talk one way with them, but have some other kind of manner of speech when you pray, it will sound phony. Avoid "churchy" language, and pray how you would talk to a friend. Model authentic prayer, and invite the student to pray in normal language and inflection. We must approach God with our true self and all of what is there—not just the "spiritual" part we deem acceptable. As C. S. Lewis wisely observed, when we pray "we must lay before [God] what is in us, not what ought to be in us."[2]

Another helpful thing to do in meetings with students is to set goals. These do not have to be huge or grandiose objectives, but should be simple steps to spur the student forward in their life. Rather than a goal like, "I'm going to reach all my classmates with the gospel," challenge the student to set this more attainable goal: "I'm going to actively listen for God's leading this week and will identify three of my classmates to pray for." Follow that in a few weeks with a measurable goal like this: "As I pray for these three students, I'm going to look for natural ways to talk about spiritual matters." Later, continue with: "I'm going to read a book about answering spiritual questions so I'm better prepared when people ask." Help the student set goals that are SMART:

---

2. C. S. Lewis, *Letters to Malcolm: Chiefly on Prayer* (New York: Harcourt, 2002), 20.

Simple (clear, one thing at a time)

Measurable (you can know if you did it or not)

Attainable (you really can do it)

Realistic (a slight stretch, not easy, but not foolish)

Timely (you set a deadline)

The final object to keep in mind during meetings is to pay attention to the work of God in the student. It is always best to discover (as well as you can) what the Spirit is doing, and to join God in that work. When you sense an openness to God in some area of the student's life or you see them wrestling with God, stay curious. Be God's eyes, ears, and voice to the student (of course, admitting your limited, human perspective). Whenever a student brings up a problem or concern, invite them to consider, "Where do you see God at work in this?" You could ask this question about some area of their life almost every time you get together; certainly it's a question to ask often.

There may be times when you have a lesson prepared, but something is so pressing on the student that you need to set aside your plans to address that issue. Be open to that. On the other hand, the student may benefit from you guiding them into the Scriptures even though they just wanted to "vent" about something; you could also suggest that the two of you handle the issue during the next time you meet one-on-one, rather than the current meeting, if postponing the topic seems appropriate. There is no clear, "always right" way to handle these issues, though our experience tells us to deal with the issue at hand (or the student may not hear anything you say because they are focused on the unaddressed problem).

telling isn't teaching

Mentoring does involve some teaching—but not as much as you might think. Most of the time, even when you're in a formal Bible study, you'll be asking questions, listening to the student, and listening for the whisper of the Holy Spirit for insight into what to do or say (or not say). As a wise old adage reminds us: "Telling isn't teaching; listening isn't learning." For mentoring to work, the student needs to be taught by your example—and when you speak, your words should be few. As you do this, you'll be doing the very things Jesus did with his disciples in the meetings he had alone with them. And with God's help, you'll witness the same transformation in a student that changed the lives of those first-century believers—and the course of history.

The Real World ...

My gift is teaching. Can't I just teach Sunday school classes for a few students and call that mentoring?

The teaching gift is a wonderful blessing from God. But using nothing but that gift in a mentoring setting is like trying to overhaul a car engine with one wrench. Go ahead and teach Sunday school, but if you choose to mentor a student, you'll have to listen more than teach, model more than talk, and ask questions more than give answers—it will require a whole-life example and commitment. Actually, we believe mentoring will help you become a better teacher.

Shouldn't we be getting the Word of God into students so they live in truth? If we let students talk all the time, they're just sharing their ignorance; what they need is more time in the Bible.

We never said they don't need the Bible; what we asked you to reflect on are effective—and ineffective—ways to go about doing that. You simply can't teach someone by "presenting"; students must be engaged. And you don't show love by making someone always listen to you. Active listening is so powerful, we actually use the phrase "*pay attention*," which underscores that it is a kind of relational *currency* that has great value.

Why do a formal Bible study at all? Can't we just have Be-With times and let God do whatever he wants when we get together?

Mentoring is helping a student become like Jesus. In order to do that, we need to know about Christ's life and teachings as found in the Gospels. In addition, Jesus used Old Testament Scripture in his teaching and recognized its importance. He also promised additional teaching that would come through his apostles, led by the Holy Spirit (John 16:12–15)—what we find in the New Testament. Something vital is missing if mentoring only becomes about you and your life, rather than connecting a student to God and his life. And God himself says we need his Word for "showing us truth, exposing our rebellion, correcting our mistakes, training us to live [his] way. Through the Word we are put together and shaped up for the tasks God has for us" (2 Tim. 3:16–17 MSG). Your grasp of the Word and studying it together will help students see the Bible fleshed out in a real person. Like Jesus did for the disciples, discussing Scripture together helps "sort out the tangles and untie the knots."

chapter summary

Verse to Remember: Mark 4:33–34

With many similar parables Jesus spoke the word to them, as much as they could understand. He did not say anything to them without using a parable. But when he was alone with his own disciples, he explained everything.

We believe truth from God's Word is a catalyst for spiritual change, and so at the heart of mentoring meetings is discussion of Scripture and scriptural principles. Mentors need to select creative material to help students understand truth in bite-sized portions with a super-sized application in daily life. When mentors meet with their students, they:

➲ Ask good questions.

➲ Listen to the student.

➲ Follow the Holy Spirit's insight when determining what to say (or not say).

A mentor looks for how God is working in the student and tries to support that work. A mentor prays for and with the student, and regularly helps the student set personal goals.

chapter 8

A Commitment to Be-With

What if you took a driver's ed class and they never let you get behind the wheel? Can you imagine being a teenager, getting keys to a brand new car, and all you've done is read a book about driving? There's no way to really learn to drive other than actually getting in the car and driving. You have to feel and experience such a skill in your hands, arms, and feet. The instructor needs to guide you, encourage you, and if necessary, step on the brake to protect you. But you have to drive.

Mentoring is a lot like that. You, the mentor, are the "life ed" instructor. Your job includes classroom instruction, but it also requires that you sit beside the student, touching the brakes now and then, letting the student do life while you guide and help.

Mentoring is instructive, but not just instruction. It's educational, but it's not school. It's learning to read—and having a student read—not a book, but *life*.

When you mentor a student, you need to make a commitment to Be-With times. These are meetings but not classes, and they are one of the most powerful means at your disposal to influence a student toward maturity and living like Jesus.

teaching in real-life settings

Let's say you wanted to instill in your student one of Jesus' core values: that it is better to serve than to be served. In other words, you want the student to see his areas of pride and to confront that self-seeking part that conforms to the world around him. You could do a Bible study on pride and hope he gets it; you could share an article on the subject; you could just bring up the topic in conversation. All good ideas. But an even better way to make this point unforgettable is to speak to the issue when the student is right in the middle of some behavior that betrays their need for correction. When the student is in the act of saying something prideful or doing something self-serving, you can point it out by telling a story or using a timely illustration (of course, lovingly, without shaming them). That's why the Be-With model is so important—you're with the student in enough situations that these things will occur, and, if you've got your mentor's radar on, you'll be able to take advantage of such teaching moments.

Jesus modeled this style of teaching with his characteristic wisdom, love, and creativity. Note the following example:

> They came to Capernaum. When he was safe at home, he asked them, "What were you discussing on the road?" [Like he didn't know!] The silence was deafening — they had been arguing with one another over who among them was greatest. He sat down and summoned the Twelve. "So you want first place? Then take the last place. Be the servant of all." He put a child in the middle of the room. Then, cradling the little one in his arms, he said, "Whoever embraces one of these children as I do embraces me, and far more than me — God who sent me."
>
> MARK 9:33–37 MSG

Because Jesus was living the Be-With lifestyle, he could take their pride-filled conversation and use it as an object lesson. He could demonstrate his point with something at hand, namely, a nearby child, and give the disciples the unforgettable image of him holding that little one as a model of true "greatness"—not the jockeying for position and power they'd been engaging in.

Notice that Jesus wasn't speaking on the topic of greatness to the masses, nor was he teaching a class. This lesson came as a result of capitalizing on a Be-With moment. Mentoring involves frequently being with a student in a variety of settings so those moments happen. Such teaching opportunities cannot be planned, but they *can* be noticed and leveraged when they occur, and they can be cultivated by intentional time spent together.

Such moments present themselves in ordinary events that one might easily overlook. They could be while driving in a car, waiting in a line, watching people interact, or talking after the game. As a wise mentor, always be on the lookout for something deeper going on in a commonplace event, or ask questions that get underneath the surface of actions or reactions you observe.

Here's another example from Jesus' life of how careful listening in an ordinary situation can lead to extraordinary breakthroughs. One time a man came up to him and asked, "Good Teacher, what must I do to inherit eternal life?" (Luke 18:18). Jesus didn't answer his question directly. And he wasn't taken in by the flattery: "Why, thank you my good man, how good of you to see my goodness!" Instead, Jesus noticed the peculiar way the man phrased his query and shot back a question in reply. Jesus pressed him: "Why do you call me *good?*" (v. 19, emphasis added). What Jesus noticed was the ease with which this man bandied about the word "good." And the crux of the man's problem was his own self-righteousness. His glib use of the word revealed the truth that he saw himself as "good" and therefore couldn't see any sin he needed to have forgiven. Jesus took the man deeper and explained to him that he needed to obey God's commandments — *he* needed to be "good" — to which the man reflexively replied that he'd done so since his youth. Think of the audacity! Here is a man in the presence of the only human being — Jesus — who actually *has* kept every commandment, and he's saying he's just as good as him. Amazing how Jesus had a laser fix on this man's real problem. Jesus could see, and wanted the man to see, that what stood in the way of his gaining eternal life was his failure to recognize his sin. And Jesus was able to expose that sin by carefully listening to how the man phrased a simple question and then pointing out the way the man's words revealed his self-deception. The *coup de grace* was Jesus asking him to give away all his money. The man's inability to do that made plain there was one commandment in particular — the most important commandment of all — he'd been flagrantly disobeying: "You shall have no other gods before me" (Deut. 5:7).

In a similar fashion, we as mentors listen to our students' words, sometimes going beyond the actual phrases to what lies beneath those words. Often that's the moment when we hear the Holy Spirit giving us supernatural insight into their inner needs. When that happens, it's an amazing blessing. Then we gently hold up a mirror for the students to see their real issues and help them work on what they've discovered.

be-with activities

So what's a typical Be-With setting? There are so many, we hardly know where to begin—because almost everything you do in life can become a Be-With time. Here are just a handful of examples so you get an idea:

Attending church

Working on a house project

Running errands

Watching a movie

Going to one of your children's activities with the student

Taking a class together

Attending a school play, game, or other event

Concerts

Going to a sporting event

Taking the student to breakfast or lunch

Going for a walk in the park

Shopping

Taking the student to your place of employment

Engaging in your hobby with the student

Day trips to nature attractions, beaches, hiking, museums, amusement parks, etc.

Talking before or after a ministry event

Exercise, runs, workouts, etc.

Yard work

Washing the car

Playing video games

Biking

Supporting the student when he or she is getting an award

One gifted youth pastor shared two of his favorite Be-With activities:

Road trips are great. I'm always on the lookout for retreat centers and places to visit for my ministry. Every time I drive to check out some potential new destination, I make it a point to invite a couple of the students I'm mentoring to come along. Not only does it provide great company and make the day more fun, I get students' impressions about the location. Best of all, we almost always have deep conversations about real life while we're driving.

The other thing I love to do are "Pull Asides." In the middle of a program, a leadership meeting, or an event of some kind, I will pull aside someone I'm mentoring and give them a quick vision talk. It could be based on something that has just happened in the program or something totally unrelated. For me, mentoring takes place all the time in the cracks of life. I have so many great stories about this kind of stuff. This past weekend, it happened again. One guy I'm mentoring just graduated and is going to school to be a microbiologist. I pulled him aside and told him that I love his brain, but I love his heart more. The microbiology thing is cool, but I think he has what it takes for ministry, and I wanted to tell him so. It was one of those talks that I think we will both remember for a long time.

be-with agenda

What should happen during your Be-With times? Here's a simple outline to help you invest well in the student. If you keep these four key words in mind, you'll maximize every opportunity: *pray, encourage, share,* and *challenge*.

First, whenever you get together, be sure you take at least a few moments to *pray*. Ideally, do this as you begin and then pray again as you end your time together. For example, "God, help us to be open today for what you have for each of us" or "God, help us to see, hear, and feel you in our time together. Teach us more about you." Also if an issue comes up, be open to stopping the conversation and turning to God on the spot for wisdom, help, or comfort. Teach the student "breath prayers" (simple prayers that happen throughout the day, like gradually expelling a deep breath), and when you say you're going to pray for them, do it right in that moment. What you're modeling to the student is how natural and conversational prayer can be, and how prayer doesn't have to be a long, drawn-out affair. Of course, like a spiritual meal, prayer "feeds" the soul, and that's a good thing too.

Second, be sure to *encourage* in generous amounts. Make your encouragement specific, and make it not only about *what* the student *does* ("Great job on that assignment; way to go bringing your friend to church; thanks for reaching out to that kid who needed to talk") but also about *who* the student is *becoming* ("I love your openness and deep desire to let God lead you in every area of your life; I see Jesus at work in you; I've noticed you becoming more compassionate"). It's no exaggeration to say that students' lives can be radically transformed by an encouraging word that comes at just the right time. These messages can have the kind of power that almost feels like God himself has just spoken using your words, and the truth goes deep into their hearts. Such messages may come back to the student years later and continue to shape their behavior and character. They become defining, internalized "gold" whose value is hard to describe but much appreciated. "A word aptly spoken is like apples of gold in settings of silver" (Prov. 25:11).

A third thing to do when you are together is to *share* your own story, your own journey with God. What is God teaching *you*? If God has impressed you with a passage of Scripture that speaks to an area of your life, share it with the student. If you're facing a tough situation ("I'm visiting my in-laws this weekend and they're not Christ-followers. I need patience to just love them and let God work!"), share that need honestly and have the student hold you up in prayer. It's important to model growth as a process: you're not mentoring the student because you've got it all together, but because you're on the *path* toward Christ-likeness. You're showing the student that there are ups and downs to the Christian life and that you, too, experience both joys and frustrations in the lifelong progression toward being "complete in Christ" (Col. 1:28 NASB). On top of that, the lessons you learn may be exactly what your student needs to learn. By sharing them, the student is blessed by the very things blessing you. (God is a master at coordinating that kind of thing!)

Finally, every meeting should include some kind of *challenge*. Look for those moments when the student is teachable, when you can tell God is up to something and you speak to that. Because you know the student, you can make your challenges very specific. Here are some examples:

- ➲ It's one thing to encourage a student to be "more loving"; it's quite another to know the very people the student is having trouble loving, and together set goals to make those relationships more God-honoring.

- ➲ It's one thing to teach about the value of caring for our bodies as the temple of the Holy Spirit (1 Cor. 6:19); it's another to help a student deal with her unhealthy eating habits or lack of exercise—and starting a workout plan together gives you yet another Be-With time.

⮑ It's one thing to teach about treating the opposite sex with respect and honor; it's another to confront a student on how his coarse language about girls and their bodies is dishonoring to his sisters in Christ.

⮑ It's one thing to urge students to be positive and maintain respect for parents and leaders; it's another to help a student take specific steps to go after their negativity and help them obey the "2:14 Principle" (from Philippians 2:14; we ask them to get their attitudes right because Paul said "Do everything without grumbling or arguing" [TNIV]).

⮑ It's one thing to encourage a student to use their gifts in service to God's kingdom; it's another to know their gifting and help them find areas to serve where they can develop those gifts.

⮑ It's one thing to commend the value of honesty; it's another to point out specific ways the student has been exaggerating or distorting truth and to call them out to complete accuracy in what they say.

We also challenge students by saying "the last 10 percent." What we mean is that sometimes we say things to another person, but for some reason there's a key point we keep inside. Maybe we're afraid, maybe we're second-guessing ourselves, maybe we tell ourselves it won't do any good, or that feelings might be hurt—but we don't say the thing that most needs to be said. And then the person walks away with only part of the story, doomed to repeat their mistake because they're unaware of some crucial feedback.

⮑ Someone who aspires to sing but really doesn't have the talent embarrasses herself at an audition because no one tells her that her talent lies elsewhere.

⮑ Someone who thinks they're helping others, but is just running off at the mouth wounds someone again because no one confronts him about his self-centered patterns of communication and failure to practice good listening.

➲ Someone thinks they're being funny, but in truth what they do is annoying, yet no one levels with them so they keep driving people away and don't know why.

When trust has been built, when love has been shown, when the student knows they will always get our honest perspective because we truly care for them, we take the risk to say the last 10 percent.

When I (Bo) received the following emails from guys I'd mentored years ago, I remembered how much I loved being in their lives. Their words reminded me of how important it is to speak the truth in love. It was the simple things I'd completely forgotten that were the very things God used to make a difference in their lives.

> Sometimes you would want to have a team activity, and you assigned us team captains to organize something for our individual teams. One time I kind of fudged it. We went to the basketball game at school, and I hung out with the guys but didn't really organize anything like I'd agreed to do. So you pulled me aside and said, "I wanted you to organize a team activity, and you didn't. Be a planner. You're not being honest with me or yourself when you blow it off." For an older man to say to a younger man, "Be honest, be a man of integrity, make sure your word is good and golden" made a profound impact on me. Thanks Bo, you helped me become a better man by being honest and telling me the truth.

And another story:

> Whatever the tough conversation, you were able to say what needed to be said and then drop it. You didn't carry a grudge. Your attitude was, "I told you, I reproved you, I expect you to listen, and I'll never bring it up again." Many leaders hold grudges. They "blacklist" people because of something done wrong. But with you, that's not the way it was. Once the situation was dealt with, you moved forward and let bygones be bygones. If someone is as big a screwup as I was, they really need forgiveness. They need a mentor who can say, "You got it, now let's move forward." I'm a better man because of how you did that for me. Thanks Bo.

Better to say "the last 10 percent," the difficult truth that may sting but will be beneficial in the end. "Faithful are the wounds of a friend, but deceitful are the kisses of an enemy" (Prov. 27:6 NASB).

spiritual disciplines

When you meet with students during Be-With times, it's also a good idea to bring up the topic of spiritual practices, or disciplines that keep your spiritual life strong (see Dallas Willard, *Spirit of the Disciplines*). Share what you're doing and encourage the student to experiment with some disciplines of their own.

One of the easiest practices to undertake is Scripture memorization. Especially when a student has brought up a struggle, or you've spoken to them during a Be-With time about something they need to work on, that's a good opportunity to identify a verse that speaks to the issue and have them memorize it. You can also practice these verses when you're together—sometimes while doing other things like driving or waiting—and before long, the student will have a number of valuable verses in their spiritual arsenal.

Other core spiritual practices are Bible reading, prayer, solitude, and journaling; and when the student is ready, try fasting, confession, silence, secret acts of service, and other disciplines. The fun thing about such practices is that you can make them up as needed. For example, if the student struggles with impatience, have them deliberately go into long lines or drive in the slow lanes of traffic to help them break the hold "hurry" has on them. Or suggest they go without TV for a week and notice what happens to them, good or bad. You can suggest a student drive without the radio on and talk to God, or spend a little time every so often listening to the sounds of nature and see what that does for their soul. Have them spend a day in silence and see what God says to them when they stop talking. Any training exercise you use to help you grow in some area is a spiritual practice, and using both tested, classic ones and inventing new ones can help the student grow.

a mentoring culture

Wes, a fifteen-year-old student, was afraid and ashamed to talk to his parents about something. Mark, his mentor, listened to Wes confess how a casual drink every now and then had turned into a full-blown drinking problem. Mark was glad he'd followed a leading he sensed from God to stop by Wes' house that afternoon. Now they were sitting on the front steps in the middle of a conversation that Mark knew was God-ordained.

Mark had been involved in Wes' life for the last six months and could tell Wes was tired of feeling guilty and hiding his problem from his parents. It was time to take the difficult step of telling the truth. As Mark repeated the words, "You can do this," Wes knew he could and that his mentor would be there for him when he did. And the time was now.

Wes took a big breath. His heart was pounding. After a quick word of prayer, they both stood up and walked into the house.

"Mom, I need to talk to you ..." Wes began.

This is mentoring.

Kate, an eighth grader, got the call to come down to the principal's office. When she saw her mom waiting there, she knew the news couldn't be good. Her mother told her that her grandmother had died that morning. Kate was shocked, and she couldn't imagine what her life would be like without her grandmother. On the drive home, she felt sad, afraid, and so alone. When they pulled up in front of the house, Kate had another surprise: there was her mentor's car in the driveway. Susan had been a part of her life for the past two years, and she was there waiting for her. Susan greeted Kate with a hug, reminding her that she would be there to walk with her through this time. She wanted Kate to know that she could count on her. Kate was so thankful to have someone to listen, not to try to fix her or give answers, but to be with her—just like her grandmother had been.

This is mentoring.

"I baptize you now in the name of the Father, and the Son, and the Holy Spirit." As Sean's father came out of the water, he immediately embraced his eighteen-year-old son. This indeed was a very special celebration.

When Sean gave his life to Christ two years ago, his dad could not believe the life-change that followed. A mentoring relationship with the youth pastor had made a big impact on Sean. There was a peace and joy that his father could clearly see—something so contagious he had to find out about it for himself. And now he was in the water next to his son, being baptized by the youth pastor who'd mentored Sean.

This is mentoring.

Pat was so excited as he tore open the letter from the Bible school he'd applied to. As he held the letter in his hands, he realized he was probably the last person anyone would have guessed would ever go to Bible school.

Three years ago, Pat didn't know who God was, nor did he care. Keith, a youth ministry volunteer, had started to get to know Pat and ultimately shared Christ with him. Keith then mentored Pat for three years. He answered his questions and listened to his struggles. He kept Pat on track and reminded him that God had a plan for his life. Now Pat was about to follow that plan by going to Bible school and pursuing full-time ministry.

Pat couldn't wait to give back to someone what he had received from Keith. He wanted to be a difference-maker and help challenge another young person, just like Keith had challenged him.

As he read, "Congratulations, you have been accepted!" he stopped and said a prayer of thanks. He couldn't wait to tell his parents—and Keith.

This is mentoring.

If you were in doubt that mentoring is a great idea or thought it might not be for you, we hope by now you've run out of excuses! Yet we cannot end this book without sharing one more dream, and that is for mentors to create a mentoring culture wherever they go. Whether it's your church, your family, your friends or co-workers, or even neighbors, why not encourage those around you to mentor students? What you do with a student will undoubtedly be a great contribution for years to come; think of the added impact of having others around you build into the lives of students as well. What about people in your small group? Others who volunteer with you? Friends and family members? Other couples who have grown children and who have so much to offer? Buy several copies of this book and pass it on to anyone who might be even slightly interested. Help them get a vision for what could happen if not just one or two students in your church were mentored—but if dozens had caring adults to love and guide them to Christian maturity. You could change your church or your neighborhood. A whole generation would be that much more ready to assume the mantle of leadership in the church and in society. We can turn back the tide of students giving in to peer pressure, not making wise decisions, getting into unhealthy relationships; and we can help students who feel lost and adrift in the world find their God-given purpose and direction. Mentoring will pave the way.

And as if all that weren't enough, those who do the mentoring are doubly blessed. You get to see the lives of students transformed *and* you get refueled yourself by having a courtside seat to what God is doing. If you're in youth ministry, nothing—*nothing*—we know of has more potential to keep you in the game of ministry than a close connection with a student or two who every year experience the power of your loving mentoring. Whatever you do in life as a profession, watching a student's life unfold as God works in them through your involvement is about the best use of your time we can think of. The *pay* may not be much, but the *payoff* is incalculable.

Our final encouragement to you is this: take a student along for the ride of your life. And invite other adults to join you in an adventure of their own through mentoring. There is a world, a generation, at risk, and they're looking for someone to show them the way.

Are *you* the one they seek to "be-with"? We believe you are. Say yes to God and to a student, then get ready for the exciting adventure of mentoring the next generation!

The Real World ...

I am still struggling with the time commitment because I'm so busy. I want to mentor a student, but I don't know if I can find enough Be-With time.

This question keeps coming up and we don't think there are any easy answers. But we must stress how valuable it is to mentor, and why, though you may not be able to *find* the time, it's worth it to *make* the time. You need to consider all your choices, not just this one. It may be that you need to be more intentional with the time that you are already spending with students. Maybe you need a reminder that mentoring is a lifestyle more than adding lots of activities. Keep trying to open your life in natural ways to a student, rather than coming up with new things that fill your schedule. Better time management may be of help. Bottom line: if you see the benefit, other things may have to go.

I feel like I'm always giving to others. When do I get replenished myself?

Great question, because this is about much more than mentoring. You need to go back to the "Grand Secret of Life" (chapter 3). No one will walk up to you and do this for you. What replenishes you? Put it on your calendar and do it, just like you had an appointment with someone. And consider if some of the draining experiences can be given to someone else, or just not done at all.

Mentoring seems to require a lot of creativity. I'm definitely not the creative type. Can I do it?

You have already taken an important step by reading this book. The creativity is not up to you: the Holy Spirit will help. The key is to listen for God's leading. All you really have to do is be open and transparent, sharing your own life. And pay attention to the student. God will speak through you in surprising ways.

What's the best time to start a mentoring relationship?

The important thing is just to start. I (Bo) personally like starting a mentoring relationship in September, right at the beginning of the school year. I do my interviews and READY process during the summer, then really dive into it in September. We go through to the end of the school year, and continue a bit more informally in the summer. I like nine months to be the finish line. For some students, I do another year, same cycle, while adding a new student or two in the fall.

I want to mentor but am still a little nervous. I wish I could watch someone so that I could feel a little more confident.

Ideally, yes, it would be great to observe a mentor in action. If you can tag along with someone who is doing it, great.

But if this is on your heart to do, don't wait just because you don't have someone to show you. Trust God and learn while you go. God may have you become that example for someone else to learn from someday. Be the first if you have to, but get in the game! It's an adventure and a privilege you won't regret. Remember, God is for you—you can do this!

chapter summary

Verse to Remember: Mark 9:33–37

They came to Capernaum. When he was in the house, he asked them, "What were you arguing about on the road?" But they kept quiet because on the way they had argued about who was the greatest. Sitting down, Jesus called the Twelve and said, "If anyone wants to be first, he must be the very last, and the servant of all." He took a little child and had him stand among them. Taking him in his arms, he said to them, "Whoever welcomes one of these little children in my name welcomes me; and whoever welcomes me does not welcome me but the one who sent me."

Mentors use everyday experiences to make connections to spiritual lessons, which is exactly what Jesus did with his disciples. Mentors are mindful of what changes a student over time, so they:

Pray—Like a spiritual meal, prayer feeds the soul.

Encourage—An encouraging word at the right time can radically transform a student.

Share—Mentors' personal lessons may be just the lessons students need to learn.

Challenge—A specific challenge during a teachable moment helps build spiritual maturity in students' lives.

Mentors are willing to say the last 10 percent, to speak with loving but frank honesty. Mentors model spiritual disciplines and encourage students to experiment with some disciplines of their own. Ideally, we need a mentoring culture to take root because the Be-With lifestyle is the most effective way to train students to be like Jesus. And, if you're a youth leader, mentoring has enormous potential to keep you in the game of ministry. The power of your loving mentoring can change a generation.

A Guide for Launching a Mentoring Relationship

six questions students need to ask about life with God

This appendix contains lesson plans and Be-With ideas for your introductory sessions with your student. We strongly recommend you purchase the companion book, *The Be-With Factor Student Guide: Six Questions Students Need to Ask About Life with God* to give to each student you mentor. Working from their own copy, the book will:

➲ Reinforce teaching, with key points in print

➲ Help discussion flow more easily, with questions right in front of the student

➲ Provide Scripture references

➲ State memory verses

➲ Clearly note spiritual exercises and assignments

➲ Allow space for journaling

Between each of the six study sessions ("Big Questions") with your student, we suggest you have a more informal Be-With time. As we've outlined below, the Be-With times have the added benefit of topically setting up the Big Question that follows. It will therefore take twelve weeks to cover this material: a Be-With time one week (which helps to set up the topic but is also just about being together) and a study time the following week (a more formal discussion on one of the six questions). By alternating this way, if you meet weekly, you will have approximately three months of themed study and Be-With times.

One aspect present in this outline that is somewhat uncharacteristic of typical Be-With meetings is that we've deliberately tied those six times to a topic. Most often in mentoring, the Be-With times stand alone without such a specific theme in mind. While Be-With times are always intentional, they don't always have to have such a tight fit with the next week's study. They should always be fun and not feel forced or like "field trips." Stay fluid and creative as you plan these Be-With times, especially as you carry them out in the future. We started the outline this way to provide a focus for you and the student as you get to know each other better, with the understanding that future Be-With experiences will come out of your relationship and fit what you're learning about the student (and the student's needs).

For all of the Be-With and Big Question study times, we give you written coaching for how to lead that meeting. That direction includes suggestions under the following headers:

Location: A specific place to meet with your student that captures the theme of the meeting (some weeks this is more important than others).

Big Idea: The overall purpose of what you want to accomplish (whatever other rabbit trails you follow, don't miss this objective).

Check In: Two or three questions to ask the student at the beginning of every meeting that will deepen your relationship and help reinforce weekly challenges.

Activity (Be-With Times): Something that is fun and relational, but can still be used as a learning experience.

Study (Discussion Questions): The list of questions and Bible references from which you choose what you will discuss with your student.

Leader's Notes: Suggestions for bringing clarity to the discussion or other coaching tips to help you mentor.

Scripture Memory: A verse suitable for memorizing, tied to the study theme, along with an application question.

Personal Challenge: A challenge or "stretch" activity that you give to the student.

My Life: Suggestions for what to do on your own between meetings, to get you and the student to journal and go deeper in your walk with God.

Relational Reminders: A place for you to jot down ideas for prayer, encouragement, and sharing what God is doing in your life.

Here are the six "Big Questions" we propose you study together as you begin the mentoring process:

1. How Does God Show Me He's Real?
2. What Does God Want from Me?
3. What Purpose Does God Have for My Life?
4. Why Does It Matter What I Believe about God?
5. How Does God Help Me Stay Strong When Life Is Hard?
6. What Kind of People Does God Want in My Life?

The meetings mentioned below come only *after* the selection process to choose the student you are to mentor (outlined in chapter 6). If you have identified your READY student and made a clear invitation that they've accepted, the next step is to schedule your first meeting together officially as mentor and student. We suggest you begin with a Be-With activity to set the stage and begin your journey together.

Be-With Activity#1
(Setup to Big Question #1)

Location: Someplace that was important to you when you were in high school, maybe even where you used to hang out with friends or play sports. You could also go to a themed restaurant that reflects your past (for example, a fifties-style diner).

Big Idea: Help the student get to know what God is doing in your life and what you were like when you were the student's age.

Activity: Show the student pictures or a scrapbook from your past, especially from your middle school/high school era, and share what life was like for you back then. If at all possible, have a picture from when you were the same age as the student.

Let the student know that even though times have changed, some things remain the same. You can relate to many of the same struggles they face; you, too, had questions and problems during that time in your life. Also talk about your spiritual uncertainties. If you were a Christian then, talk about how you came to faith and what it was like to try to live it out at that age. If you weren't a Christian, be sure to fast-forward the story to how you came to faith later, and how God answered some of the questions and longings from your student years (at the next meeting you'll go into more detail on how you became a Christ-follower, but share the highlights here).

A great thing to share is your response to this statement: "If I could go back to the person in this picture (you as a teen), and tell him/her something I know now, it would be _____."

Remember, this is not a Bible study, but if a passage of Scripture seems to capture the essence of your story, share that verse if you can weave it in naturally.

Also share what you like to do now: what are your passions, your hobbies, the things that breathe life into you? Talk about your family, friends, what work you do outside the home, or what work you do in your home. Let down your guard and have fun. Let the student know you have a fully-orbed life that isn't just about "spiritual" things. If you're able to do so, talk about what seem to be the main "themes" of your life — issues that come up repeatedly for you. Do not preach; just share from your heart. You are modeling what you want the student to do — share openly and honestly, building bridges of understanding and identification between your world and the student's.

Also ask about the student's interests, hobbies, musical tastes, and family situation. While you're going to go into more depth in the next meeting, get an idea of their story and who God has made them to be.

We'll provide space for you to make notes in advance of your meeting times, to write down what you might want to cover in these four areas for each lesson outline. We'll also suggest a challenge that fits with the lesson (see below), but do remember to pay attention in the moment: what you pray for, encourage, share, and challenge are best spoken in response to something you see right then and there. It would be preferable to lean into those promptings of the Spirit (even if you wrote down something else before you met). Of course, these four activities may not happen in this order and shouldn't all be clustered at the end of your meeting (except for the challenge, which *does* come then). But we group them all here as a reminder at the end of the lesson plan, to make sure you did these at some time when you were together.

➲ Pray

➲ Encourage

⊃ Share

⊃ Challenge
Suggestion for this week's challenge: Ask two adults what they wish they knew at your age.

Mentor's "Every-Meeting" Checklist

Remember, every time you get together with your student, do these four things (see chapter 8):

❑ Pray (Brief prayers are fine.)

❑ Encourage (Say something specific and positive about the student. Example: "I like how attentive you were when I was talking; you're a good listener.")

❑ Share (Bring yourself — your *real* self — and God's latest work in you. Example: "I have been really impatient lately and realize I need to ask God to help me in this area before I do even more damage.")

❑ Challenge (A goal or simple action step to take this week. Example: "Do a kind thing for someone this week in such a way they don't know you did it." It's a good idea to call or email your student during the week to remind them about the challenge and see how they are doing with it.)

Big Question #1: How Does God Show Me He's Real?

Big Idea: God wants a personal relationship with us and has taken steps to make himself known.

check in

> **leader's note**
>
> Begin each time together with a brief "check in" which consists of variations on two or three questions: two are presented below, the third, about journaling, will be added when there are formal discussion meetings (not Be-With times).

1. How are you doing—*really?*
2. How did the personal challenge from last week go? If you used it, ask, "What did you find out from the two adults about what they wished they knew at your age?"

study (discussion questions)

> **leader's note**
>
> The study each week consists of a series of questions that begin with general topics, then require deeper thought, involve personal storytelling, and have the student search the Scriptures. You should answer the questions yourself after the student has shared — it's all part of letting the student in on your life and perspective. These questions are meant to stimulate discussion, not to be "test questions" to answer correctly. Most weeks, we give you more questions than you could cover in an hour. We do that deliberately so you can pick among the questions for the ones you think will best fit your student. You could also suggest the student answer the remaining questions between meetings, during reflection times alone with God. When you're together, don't get bogged

down or discouraged trying to handle every question we include. Remember, in mentoring, it's not the material you cover — it's what you *uncover* together that's important.

1 What are some of your earliest memories of what you thought God was like?

2 How has your view of God changed since then?

Read Psalm 8:3–4; 19:1–4; Romans 1:20.

3 How would you sum up what these verses are saying about God's message to humanity through his creation?

4 How does God use his creation to speak to you personally?

leader's note

Theologians call this kind of revelation "general revelation" — how God indirectly shows himself and "speaks" to all humanity at all times, contrasting it with "special revelation" — how God speaks directly to specific people at specific times, through Scripture and most dramatically through the incarnation of Jesus (see next question).

God also speaks to us through the Bible, his written Word, and Jesus, his Word (message) made flesh. Read John 1:1–5 and Hebrews 1:1–3.

5 What do these passages teach us about Jesus' role in helping us understand God?

---

leader's note

General revelation is powerful, but not sufficient; it's informative and convicting, but not redemptive; it can lead us to knowledge of sin, but not to knowledge of a Savior. That's why we need special revelation, and why Jesus is so important in God's redemptive plan. Now that he has come, we have full knowledge of what God is like, what he requires, and how he saves us. This is such good news, that we're not left groping in the dark. But there is a warning as well: "How shall we escape if we ignore such a great salvation?" (Heb. 2:3).

Now read John 1:10–14. Many people saw and heard Jesus without being changed. In our day, too, lots of people know some facts about Jesus but are not among his followers.

6 According to verses 12–13, how does someone go from being a creature *made* by God to a child *born* of God?

7 Tell the story of when and how that happened for you.

leader's note

Let the student tell how they became a Christ-follower; you already shared your story during your first Be-With time. Also listen carefully for the possibility that the student isn't sure about their relationship with God, and may either need the plan of salvation spelled out clearly, or assurance of that relationship.

Read what Jesus said in John 10:10 (especially the last half of the verse).

8 What do you think keeps some people who follow Christ from having "life to the full" as he promised?

9 What do you think is your role in making sure you experience the kind of abundant life Christ wants for you on a day-to-day basis?

10 Read John 15:5–9. Summarize in your own words the analogy Jesus used to explain this concept.

leader's note

The full life Christ promises comes from staying connected to him and obeying his instructions with a submissive heart. Some people err on the side of seeing Jesus as a taskmaster who bosses us around; others care little for any of his specific instructions and tend to be careless about following his ways.

➲ They might be ignorant of his commands, which requires learning.

➲ They might be resistive to his commands, which requires trust.

➲ They might be rebellious against his commands, which requires confronting their disobedience.

The key to experiencing the life Christ intended is to abide in him, to yield to the Holy Spirit, and to obey him, not to earn love, but in a grateful spirit of love.

scripture memory

"I have come that they may have life, and have it to the full."

JOHN 10:10

how I see this verse applying to my life:

leader's note

We include a memory verse tied to each lesson's theme. Be sure the student understands what it means and how it applies to their life. For example, after reading the verse, you could ask, "How would you use this verse in helping a friend?" or "How does this verse speak to a question people have or give God's perspective on an issue?" Or even simply ask, "How does this verse apply to your life?" as suggested in the Student Guide.

personal challenge

Suggestion for this week's challenge: Show someone grace—undeserved kindness—as a way to deepen your own experience of God's grace; when someone at school speaks unkindly to you, count to ten and picture God loving and understanding this person; respond to your parents or a teacher quickly and without questioning or resistance; think of someone who irritates you and do a simple kind act for that person.

my life

> **leader's note**
>
> After each study time, we will offer suggestions for you to give the student to meet alone with God or to do some other activity to reinforce an aspect of the study. If they're not doing so, it will be a great way to get them into the habit of journaling, and we urge you to do these exercises as well. This is one more way to share your life, through journaling about some of the same things during the week.

This week, notice the ordinary ways God reveals himself to you through nature, people, your conscience, and quiet promptings in your mind. At the end of each day, jot down how he showed you he was real that day. Be prepared to share your thoughts at the next meeting when we discuss "Big Question #2: What Does God Want from Me?"

Mentor's "Every-Meeting" Checklist

❏ Pray

❏ Encourage

❏ Share

❏ Challenge

Be-With Activity#2
(Setup to Big Question #2)

Location: A bookstore or library

Big Idea: People have done great things that have changed the world for the better, and God wants to do great things in your life if you are willing to dream on a large scale.

Check In:
1. How are you doing—*really?*
2. How did the personal challenge from last week go? If you used it, ask, "What was it like to show someone kindness they didn't necessarily deserve?"

Activity: Meet at a bookstore that has a refreshment area in it (or the library if you don't have such a bookstore). Browse through the biographies of great men and women (and at least one somewhat unusual character or eccentric for the fun of it); talk about what you discover.

Possible Reflection Questions: [These should come up naturally as part of the conversation, not like you're quizzing the student and looking for a "right" answer.]

1. Is greatness just a matter of luck?
2. What kinds of qualities do great people seem to have in common?
3. What changes for the better that show up in our lives today came through people who took a stand in the past?
4. Are great people just egomaniacs or arrogant overachievers in disguise?
5. What price do you have to pay to make a difference for others?
6. Do you think God could ever use you to make a great contribution? Why or why not?

7. What are some everyday things you can do to make a difference right now in someone's life? How might that be considered a great contribution on God's behalf?

Suggestion for this week's challenge: Identify one quality of someone you admire and think about how this quality could show up more in your life; actually try to make a small change in that direction.

Mentor's "Every-Meeting" Checklist

❑ Pray

❑ Encourage

❑ Share

❑ Challenge

Big Question #2: What Does God Want from Me?

Big Idea: Christianity is about a relationship with God based on grace and love; we obey him out of gratitude, not because we legalistically keep his rules out of fear.

check in

1. How are you doing—*really*?
2. Did any interesting things come up in your journaling this week? Read or share a few thoughts from your journal.

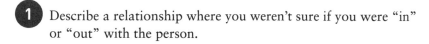

leader's note

Journaling is a very *private* practice, so be sensitive to insisting that too much personal information be shared. Allow the student freedom to share as much — or as little — as they feel comfortable disclosing.

3. How did the personal challenge from last week go? If you used it, ask, "What quality of a great person did you pick? How did you try to live that out?"

study (discussion questions)

1 Describe a relationship where you weren't sure if you were "in" or "out" with the person.

2 Why is it so hard to be close to someone who doesn't let you know where you stand with them?

Some people think a relationship with God is like that: he never lets you know where you stand, and at any moment he could turn on you if you step out of line. At times, you may also feel like you're not much of a friend to God.

3 Why does this kind of uncertainty keep us from a close relationship with him?

leader's note

The gospel is grace, precisely because the only other alternative is earning your own way to God — and that's impossible. If we keep relating to God unsure of his love or acceptance, we are doomed to a superficial and fear-based relationship. If we know we're forgiven, we can approach him with confidence and love, not trying to get something, but knowing we have what we need. We also need to know that whenever we're not at our best, he still loves and accepts us. Otherwise, we tend to "hide" when we're not doing well — another way the Evil One keeps us from fellowship with God, which is the very thing we need most when we're wandering.

4 Read John 10:11–15. What do you think Jesus wants his sheep to feel toward their shepherd?

> **leader's note**
>
> The bottom line here is that Jesus is *for* us, was willing to die for us, and desires to protect and shepherd us.

5 Read John 10:27–30. According to Jesus, whose hands are on every one of his sheep?

6 Why do you suppose Jesus stressed how secure his sheep are?

> **leader's note**
>
> Jesus' hands are on us, and the Father's hands are around his. Knowing we are secure helps us relate to God out of security, not according to our performance.

Reflect on this brief story: Once there was a tough coach who made a lot of demands on his players. He didn't seem to care about the team, and no one liked him. He would leave notes for his players, telling them what they'd done wrong and giving them lists of things he wanted them to do differently. The players would try to follow the coach's directions, but it always seemed like a lot of work, and they were constantly criticized for falling short.

Halfway through the season, that coach left and a new coach was hired in his place. The new guy was a strong coach but didn't demean the players. He was able to call the best out of the team, and he also generously encouraged them and really cared for each player. Everybody loved the new coach and they were glad to be rid of the old one.

One day, just before the last game of the season, a player found one of the old coach's "to do" notes in the back of his locker. He felt his face get hot with anger as he remembered what it was like to play under that tyrant, trying to please him to no avail. Yet as he read the note and its requirements, he realized that all the things the previous coach had written that he should do, *he was actually now doing.* He was playing harder than he'd ever played under the old coach, but he actually *wanted* to do those things on the list because of his trust, respect, and love for the new coach, and out of appreciation for how he was treated.

7 What parallels can you make to this story and to how we relate to God?

8 Read Luke 18:10–14. What light does this shed on how people act when they think their relationship with God is based on performance rather than forgiveness and grace?

9 Have you ever pretended to be righteous or been fake? Why did you think you had to do that?

---

leader's note

Pride and judgment are the fruit of religious self-righteousness. Humility and true closeness to God come from a broken and contrite heart (Ps. 51). People who think they *are* acceptable move toward pride; people who know they've been graciously *given* acceptance are grateful and humble.

Some people once asked Jesus, "What must we do to do the works God requires?" Jesus answered, "The work of God is this: to believe [that is, to trust] in the one he has sent" (John 6:28–29). The Greek word for "believe" in this passage includes the idea of "trust in, rely on, and cling to" (the New Testament was first written in Greek).

10 In light of the meaning of this verse, what is the "first order of business" between God and us, according to Jesus?

11 Why do we miss the mark if we try to follow the Ten Commandments or do other good things without first putting our trust in God's acceptance of us in Christ?

leader's note

A child who is sure of her parents' love acts very differently than a child looking for that love. A child of God who trusts in him and then obeys is vastly different from one trying to obey him, hoping that such obedience will produce acceptance.

scripture memory

Jesus answered, "The work of God is this: to believe in the one he has sent."

JOHN 6:29

how I see this verse applying to my life:

leader's note

Make sure the student has made the connection between this verse and "real life."

personal challenge

Suggestion for this week's challenge: How can you change a bad attitude you have by leaning more into the grace of God? How might just spending time with him, not "trying harder," be of help to you?

my life

Reflect on these questions: "What is an area in which I have trouble trusting God? Why is trust hard for me in that area?" Be prepared to share your thoughts at the next meeting when we discuss "Big Question #3: What Purpose Does God Have for My Life?"

Mentor's "Every-Meeting" Checklist

❑ Pray

❑ Encourage

❑ Share

❑ Challenge

Be-With Activity #3
(Setup to Big Question #3)

Location: A cemetery or an old run-down building

Big Idea: A reminder of life's brevity, emphasizing the need for an ongoing vision for my life's purpose.

Check In:
1. How are you doing—*really?*
2. How did the personal challenge from last week go? If you used it, ask, "How did leaning into grace—just spending time with God—help with any bad attitude you identified?"

Activity: Stop by a cemetery or an old building and walk around. Talk together about what you imagine these people were (or the building was) like in their/its prime. The truth about this world is that things look permanent, but they are not. Buildings and bodies—even cities and civilizations—may look like they're going to last, but they will all pass away *without exception.* Only our souls are eternal. Whatever we do with our lives, we need to act in light of what is eternal.

Possible Reflection Questions: [Remember that these should come up naturally as part of the conversation.]
1. Why do you think God made the universe in such a way that everything decays, including us?
2. Do you think most people live their lives as if they're going to die one day? Why or why not?
3. (If at a building) What do you think the architect and builders would say if they could see this now?
4. (If at a cemetery) Walk up and down the rows and notice the headstones; pick one with an inscription that looks interesting to you and explain why.

5. Knowing bodies (and buildings) decay, what do you think a person can do with their life to make it worthwhile? What do *you* want to do with your life that will count for eternity?

Suggestion for this week's challenge: Do or say something that has the potential to really make a difference—something that will *last*. It could be as simple as a note of encouragement, contacting your grandparents to see how they're doing, turning off the TV and praying for a friend, being a volunteer at church or school, etc.

Mentor's "Every-Meeting" Checklist

❏ Pray

❏ Encourage

❏ Share

❏ Challenge

Big Question #3: What Purpose Does God Have for My Life?

Big Idea: God has plans and desires for your life, and you're free to "dream big" because a big God wants to work through you.

check in

1. How are you doing—*really*?
2. Did any interesting things come up in your journaling this week? Read or share a few thoughts from your journal.
3. How did the personal challenge from last week go? If you used it, ask, "What activity did you do that you hoped would make a difference?" (By the way, don't be discouraged if you saw no immediate results; cultivate this as a lifestyle, not as a quick fix to problems.)

study (discussion questions)

1 Describe a time when you saw or tried to use a tool that you couldn't figure out how to use correctly.

2 What was it like when someone who knew what they were doing used the tool?

leader's note

This discussion sets up the idea that our lives are like a tool in God's hands. When we try to live our lives without God's guidance and leadership, we're not using the tool according to design. But once God, the master Craftsman, has us in his hands and we allow him to use us, we fulfill our very reason for being. *Don't try to bring all this out as the student answers this question*; it's just a setup for that idea to naturally suggest itself as the rest of the discussion unfolds.

3 Read Isaiah 64:8. Knowing God made you as he did, what are some of the unique aspects of you, his special "pottery," that might indicate the plans he has for you and what he wants to do through your life?

leader's note

This is a great time to speak into the student's life. Your words of agreement and affirmation after the student has shared what he or she sees may well be remembered for a lifetime.

Read Ephesians 2:10. The word for "workmanship" is the same root word that's behind the English word "poem."

4 What's your reaction to the idea that you are God's poem?

5 In the last part of Ephesians 2:10, it mentions that God has given much thought beforehand to the good works you will do. What does that advance preparation for your life mean to you personally?

---

leader's note

Don't get sidetracked by a conversation on the subject of predestination, which may come up here. The point of the question is that God has given great care and thought to your life and created you with a design in mind. You're certainly not a puppet, and it is your job to find the unique way he has wired you so you can cooperate with what he intends for you to do in the world. This is also a time to let your student know ways they can dream big dreams about what God may have in store for them.

Read Jeremiah 29:11. In that context, Israel was in exile far from home, but God was letting them know their hard times were not going to last.

6 Because God's heart is the same toward you, how would you put into your own words, using your own name, the promise that is being given to you through the prophet Jeremiah?

"Come, follow me," Jesus once said to some men who'd been trying to catch some fish, "and I will send you out to fish for people" (Mark 1:17 TNIV). Jesus had a big change in mind for them. Notice that Jesus' role is to help us become certain kinds of people. Where we are, or what job we're doing is not as important as who we are and what kind of character we're developing. Notice Paul's words: "It is God's will that you should be sanctified: that you should avoid sexual immorality"

(1 Thess. 4:3); he also wrote a little later, "Be joyful always; pray continually, give thanks in all circumstances, for this is God's will for you in Christ Jesus" (5:16–18). Now read all those verses aloud, but after the word "you," insert your name.

7 If someone asked you, "What is God's will for me?" what do these verses say is part of the answer?

---

leader's note

Students often want to know God's will for their lives, which in their minds usually boils down to what college they should go to, who they will marry, and what career they should choose. But if they instead take the approach that they should do God's will as revealed in Scripture (obey his commands) and look to how he gifted them — what their longings and desires are — they will most likely find answers to all those other questions in their *preferences*, not in some voice from heaven. When we're obedient to God, our preferences usually *are* his will (see next question)!

---

8 Read Psalm 37:4. If the "desires of your heart" are what God wants to give you, then what does that say about an important part of how to find God's will for your life?

9 The famous fifth-century Christian leader Augustine once wrote, "Love God, and do as you please." How does that teaching line up with this verse? Can that be taken too far? Explain.

10 Read Luke 16:10. Based on this teaching, if you wanted greater responsibilities or "advancement" in God's kingdom, what should you do first? Why do you think God set it up that way?

How do you think this applies to God's leading you into the next step of his plan for your life?

leader's note

It's very important for students to do well the things required of life in the present, as prerequisites for future blessings. How they treat brothers and sisters now prepares them to treat their spouses well. How they treat teachers and parents now prepares them to follow their future boss' leadership. Resisting telling white lies now trains them for keeping their integrity when it will really matter. How they do their homework, which may seem trivial, is where they develop the character to do the coming assignments from God, which could change the world. There is no wasted experience in life if we act unto the Lord. Learning to do the small things is how we learn to do the important things to come. This is where your mentoring example is so key as they see you living this out, doing everything "as working for the Lord" (Col. 3:23).

scripture memory

"For I know the plans I have for you," declares the LORD, "plans to prosper you and not to harm you, plans to give you hope and a future."

JEREMIAH 29:11

how I see this verse applying to my life:

> **leader's note**
>
> Make sure the student has made the connection between this verse and "real life."

personal challenge

Suggestion for this week's challenge: Notice something the student does well; encourage the student to step out and put that skill or character quality to even better use and to raise it a notch higher. Email or write your student a letter of encouragement, saying specifically what qualities you see in them, and then give them the note later in the week.

my life

Write a prayer asking God to show you some of the dreams he has for your life. Also, let God know some of the dreams you have in your own heart that you want to do for him. Be prepared to share your thoughts at the next meeting when we discuss "Big Question #4: Why Does It Matter What I Believe about God?"

Mentor's "Every-Meeting" Checklist

❏ Pray

❏ Encourage

❏ Share

❏ Challenge

Be-With Activity #4
(Setup to Big Question #4)

Location: A movie theater or at home with a rented movie

Big Idea: What you believe shapes how you live, for better or for worse.

Check In:
1. How are you doing—*really?*
2. How did the personal challenge from last week go? If you used it, ask, "Was there any way you were able to put to even better use the skill or character quality you spoke of last time?"

Activity: Watch a movie about a famous person to show how their beliefs shaped their life; they could be Christians (Eric Liddel in *Chariots of Fire* or C. S. Lewis in *Shadowlands* or Captain Ernest Gordon and the other POWs in *To End All Wars*) or non-Christians (the movie *Ghandi* is a good example of someone affected by some of Christ's teaching even though he wasn't a Christian; also movies like *Remember the Titans, Rudy,* or *Hoosiers*). Another option is to watch a movie about someone who starts well but eventually fails, to show how false beliefs/values lead to a wasted life (for example, Howard Hughes as portrayed in *The Aviator*). Set up the movie by telling the student to watch for the beliefs that shaped the character's life. Don't forget to make some popcorn or a favorite snack, and have fun!

Possible Reflection Questions:
1. What right beliefs helped the hero, or, what wrong beliefs led to tragedy?
2. Some beliefs seem to matter more than others. What beliefs did characters in the movie emphasize as important (even if they weren't really)?

3. Give some examples of how wrong beliefs as seen in the movie have negative consequences in life.

4. How would you react to the claim that it doesn't matter *what* you believe about God as long as you believe in him—even if your god isn't anything like the God of the Bible?

Suggestion for this week's challenge: Notice a belief that is prevalent all around you, in movies, TV, songs, etc., which is wrong yet still tends to pull you in or tempts you. Come up with a strong, succinct statement in your own words that contradicts that bad influence. For example, magazines typically show that you are acceptable only if you are beautiful and often give the impression that most people are super skinny, which is statistically wrong and emotionally harmful. The countering statement might be "God made us all different shapes and sizes, and I'm beautiful on the outside—and the inside—just the way I am."

Mentor's "Every-Meeting" Checklist

❏ Pray

❏ Encourage

❏ Share

❏ Challenge

Big Question #4: Why Does It Matter What I Believe about God?

Big Idea: Spiritual beliefs have a direct correlation to how we live our lives, so it's important to examine our core beliefs to line them up with truth.

check in

1. How are you doing—*really*?
2. Did any interesting things come up in your journaling this week? Read or share a few thoughts from your journal.
3. How did the personal challenge from last week go? If you used it, ask, "What statement did you think of to contradict a false belief in the world?"

study (discussion questions)

1 Take exactly two minutes to write down as many words as you can to describe God. After you've done that, circle one or two of the words you think are most important.

2 How would your life be different if God were not really this way?

3 Read Matthew 7:24–29. Give an example of what Jesus is talking about.

4 If Jesus and his words are so indispensable, how do you explain non-Christians whose lives seem to be going well?

leader's note

The key difference Jesus points out between the two houses is the *test* — the storm that is to come. And it will come; if not in this life, then on judgment day. Some people look good now on the out-side, but when their lives are tested, what's inside will be revealed. People who've planned and built their whole lives ignoring God's instructions and arrogantly leaving him out of the equation will cower in shame when all is revealed before the throne — no matter how "together" they seem to us now.

5 Read and then summarize in your own words what Jesus is warning us about in Matthew 24:4–5 and verses 23–26. What are some examples of false Christs and false prophets in our day who make false spiritual claims or lead people astray in the name of religion?

leader's note

False Christs don't have to be cult leaders, though such people cer-tainly qualify. They could be people or books that distort Christ and his message. In that sense, even a friend who draws you away from the Lord is acting as an "antichrist" (2 John 7).

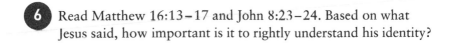

6 Read Matthew 16:13–17 and John 8:23–24. Based on what Jesus said, how important is it to rightly understand his identity?

One writer said there are basically four options for who Jesus was, historically speaking: he was either a liar (he made false claims for himself and knew it), a lunatic (made false claims for himself and really believed them), a legend (he never existed at all), or the Lord (God among us, just as he claimed).

7 Based on Jesus' words, what might he say to someone who claimed, "I believe Jesus was a good man or maybe a prophet, but nothing more"?

leader's note

People are tempted to relegate the identity of Jesus to mere theological speculation, but Jesus was abundantly clear that he must be accepted for *who he is*, and that to fail to do so imperils our very soul. Paul reiterated that there are "other Jesuses" to be rejected (2 Cor. 11:4), and the Jesus of popular opinion, or as redefined in a cult group (a good man or prophet, but nothing more) is just such a false Christ who cannot save.

When religious leaders had a wrong view of the afterlife, Jesus corrected them and said, "You are in error because you do not know the Scriptures or the power of God" (Matt. 22:29).

8 What two things led them into spiritual error, according to Jesus?

How do these two things contribute to spiritual error in our day?

---

leader's note

Jesus rebuked their wrong understanding of the Scriptures (what they taught about the afterlife) and their refusal to see how powerful God is (that he actually could bring the dead back to life and resolve the petty logical dilemmas they put forth as proof the afterlife was impossible). Because of these two misunderstandings, they developed a wrong view of life and death. Putting it positively, when we understand the Scriptures correctly and have a wide view of how truly powerful God is, we will be much less likely to fall into serious theological error.

Someone has said, "Your 'testimony' is not what you were like before you became a Christ-follower; that's your history. Your testimony is how God is for you *all the time*." Go back to your list of words you made about God in question two.

10 What words would you choose to describe the ways you sense God is personally *for* you? How important is it for you to see God this way?

scripture memory

"I told you that you would die in your sins; if you do not believe that I am he, you will indeed die in your sins."

JOHN 8:24 TNIV

how I see this verse applying to my life:

> **leader's note**
>
> Make sure the student has made the connection between this verse and "real life."

personal challenge

Suggestion for this week's challenge: Identify something that might be an idol for you—you pay too much attention to it, trust it too much, or have a wrong amount of affection for it. Consider how you can surrender that and allow God to have his rightful place again.

my life

Jesus clearly wants us to be immersed in the Scriptures and keenly aware of God's power (Matt. 22:29) so we can live well and be close to him. What are some ways you can increase your exposure to and appreciation for God's Word? Also, several times throughout the week, note a different aspect of God's power that you observe or value. Write down what you see and what it means to you. Be prepared to share your thoughts at the next meeting when we discuss "Big Question #5: How Does God Help Me Stay Strong When Life Is Hard?"

Mentor's "Every-Meeting" Checklist

❑ Pray

❑ Encourage

❑ Share

❑ Challenge

Be-With Activity #5
(Setup to Big Question #5)

Location: A shopping mall

Big Idea: Temptations are all around us in various forms and shouldn't take us by surprise.

Check In:
1. How are you doing—*really?*
2. How did the personal challenge from last week go? If you used it, ask "What possible 'idol' did you find in your life? What is your plan to let God be God?"

Activity: Go to a shopping mall. Tell the student you're just going to take a silent walk from one end to the other, and the point is just to be observant. What are the different sights, sounds, and smells you experience? When you are finished with your silent walk, also ask what the student saw, heard, and smelled. Take the conversation one step further and ask, "How many times, and in what ways were you tempted?" Be sure to go by stores like Victoria's Secret, a chocolate or candy store, a video store, an expensive jewelry store, Abercrombie, Hot Topic, Sharper Image, etc. Be honest yourself about what tempted you, to model the kind of honesty you want from the student.

Possible Reflection Questions:
1. What was an obvious temptation you experienced? What was a not-so-obvious one?
2. How do you think a person can be careful to guard purity of mind in a world like ours?
3. Imagine Jesus taking the same walk we just took. What might he react to?

Suggestion for this week's challenge: What do you anticipate will tempt you this week? Ask yourself why this tempts you—what inner need drives this temptation? Pray specifically, asking God to help fill that need in a different, healthy way, and know that your mentor will be praying as well.

Mentor's "Every-Meeting" Checklist

❑ Pray

❑ Encourage

❑ Share

❑ Challenge

Big Question #5: How Does God Help Me Stay Strong When Life Is Hard?

Big Idea: We all have areas of temptation or weakness, and if we do not watch out for them, they will sideline us; we must know what those areas are and be vigilant to guard ourselves.

check in

1. How are you doing—*really?*
2. Did any interesting things come up in your journaling this week? Read or share a few thoughts from your journal.
3. How did the personal challenge from last week go? If you used it, ask, "Were you able to figure out what was driving your temptations? Did praying help? How?"

study (discussion questions)

(Read this first paragraph before asking the questions.) Experience shows we tend to sin in four big areas:

➲ Relational breakdowns (including lying, cheating, gossip, anger, excluding someone)

➲ Sexual misconduct (with a boyfriend/girlfriend, pornography, crass language and jokes)

➲ Financial wrongdoing (stealing, cheating, selfishness, materialism, greed)

➲ Addictions (drugs, alcohol, partying, eating disorders, perfectionism)

While there are several variations under each of these categories, we human beings tend to have our "fatal flaws" in these broad areas. We may not sin in any dramatic way, but lots of little compromises can add up to much pain and shame. If a person eventually does trash their life, it will usually follow one of these paths.

Relational breakdowns come in many flavors: explosive anger, betrayal of trust, disloyalty, abandonment, selfishness, using others for your own advantage, and jealousy, to name a few.

1 Pick one of these breakdowns that you've experienced in some relationship in your life, either done to you or that you did to someone else, and tell what happened.

2 What was the eventual outcome of that breakdown?

Read Proverbs 7:21–27. This passage describes in poetic—and somewhat graphic—detail, sexual misconduct and its aftermath. Verse 21 describes one aspect of how seduction works, and verse 25, another. If you want to stay pure, it's much easier to avoid what comes *before* the act of sex than trying to stop sexual activity after passions are inflamed.

3 What are those two "pre-sexual" activities to steer clear of?

4 Have you ever used or had these used on you? Explain.

leader's note

What we're getting after here is that flirting and fantasies precede sexual sin. Before you actually put your body in a compromising situation, you have used words and allowed your heart to go there. The way to avoid sexual immorality is to first avoid the kind of people who lure you with their words. You must also protect your heart and your thought life because your actions will follow whatever your mind fixates on. The young man in Proverbs needed to avoid getting taken in by the woman's sexually charged words, and he needed to not allow his heart and mind to imagine the scenario which eventually came to pass. It also goes without saying that we should never be the kind of people who use words like that to seduce someone we're not married to, nor should we ever intentionally — or even carelessly — contribute to weakening the resolve of a boyfriend or girlfriend through our dress or other actions.

5 Now, let's move on to financial wrongdoing. While outright theft may not be common among those you know, what are some ways greed, credit card misuse, copyright violations, or materialism can cause problems?

leader's note

Money problems are not about money: they reveal character weaknesses, most commonly the refusal to delay gratification. Beyond that, people use material things to comfort, excite, and otherwise distract them from the pain in life. In that sense, a person can become "addicted" to the pleasurable feelings associated with acquisition (a shopaholic). The tenth commandment is about coveting, and using credit to buy what you cannot afford is a violation of that command — not to mention terrible stewardship and a form of enslavement. Help students see that a wrong relationship to "things" will cause untold pain and heartache, while keeping possessions in their rightful place brings enormous freedom.

Let's propose a hypothetical future in which you reject God and choose to cast off all moral restraints.

6 Go through each of the four areas mentioned at the beginning of this lesson and share what might be your most self-destructive tendency:

➲ Relational breakdowns

➲ Sexual misconduct

➲ Financial wrongdoing

➲ Addictions

If combating character weaknesses were easy, we'd all be successful at it. But the Bible is clear these matters are a struggle—at times, it's like a war.

7 Read the following verses. At the end of each set of verses put into your own words how God helps us as we fight this fight against sin:

➲ John 15:5

➲ Romans 12:1–2; 13:12–14

➲ 1 Corinthians 6:18–20; 10:13

➲ Galatians 5:13–18

➲ Hebrews 13:5–7

⊃ James 4:7–8

⊃ 1 Peter 5:5–9

8 Do you know any verses not on this list that help you resist
temptation? What are they?

9 The best of us will sometimes fall and commit the very sins we
detest. What do the following verses teach we should do when
that happens?

⊃ Proverbs 24:16

---

leader's note: Get up again!

⊃ James 5:16

---

leader's note: Confess wrongdoing and bring it into community
— tell a person, not just God.

⊃ 1 John 1:8–2:2

---

leader's note: Know that God has promised to wipe away not
just past sin, but all sin; we can be honest because God knows our
sinfulness and invites us to own and confess it. Then we can walk
in fellowship with him, being continually cleansed day by day,
moment by moment.

scripture memory

> If we confess our sins, he is faithful and just and will forgive us our sins and purify us from all unrighteousness.
>
> 1 JOHN 1:9

how I see this verse applying to my life:

> **leader's note**
>
> Make sure the student has made the connection between this verse and "real life."

personal challenge

Suggestion for this week's challenge: Focus on a good quality that counteracts your fatal flaw. How can you exercise and strengthen it this week? Be aware of what triggers your fatal flaw. What steps can you take to keep from getting into a fatal flaw situation?

my life

Reflect on what would happen if you gave in to the "fatal flaw" you struggle with. What might your life look like in five years if you don't hold this flaw at bay? Write out a vivid description of your life trapped and dominated by that sin. Contrast that description with another portrait of your life completely and utterly free from that flaw—what might it look and feel like if you could stop it now? Remember, as a Christ-follower you have been promised God's help to live life more freely and more fully. Be prepared to share your thoughts at the next meeting when we discuss "Big Question #6: What Kind of People Does God Want in My Life?"

> **leader's note**
>
> For your next Be-With time, you're going to do something that will require the student to wear clothes that might get ruined. Be sure to let the student know this now, in advance.

Mentor's "Every-Meeting" Checklist

❑ Pray

❑ Encourage

❑ Share

❑ Challenge

Be-With Activity #6
(Setup to Big Question #6)

Location: You determine

Big Idea: Create a "follow the leader" scenario to show the student how bad company corrupts good behavior.

Check In:
1. How are you doing—*really*?
2. How did the personal challenge from last week go? If you used it, ask, "What good quality did you focus on to counteract the pull of your fatal flaw?"

Activity: Remember, *before* this activity, tell the student to come dressed in clothes that could be ruined (a phone-call reminder the night before might be a good idea). Then when you get together, say that you're going to play "follow the leader." Explain that the student must do exactly what you do. Come up with some fun and bizarre actions, like walking through mud, eating something that doesn't taste good (onions, hot sauce), walking through sprinklers, jumping into a pool with clothes on, etc. Do some things guaranteed to make you both laugh, but nothing humiliating or painful.

When the game is over, make the point that we can be made to do a lot of weird things just because someone we trust asks us to; how much more are we influenced by our closest friends and what they might want to do and want us to do with them (or what we might want to do to be accepted by them)?

Possible Reflection Questions:
1. What made you willing to do the crazy things I asked you to do?
2. What's the good part of peer pressure? What's the bad part?
3. What's something crazy someone urged you to do that you now wish you hadn't? Looking back, why do you think you gave in?

Suggestion for this week's challenge: Notice this week when someone asks you to do something you know is not right, and you aren't comfortable doing it. Trust in your instincts and make a stand (it may not be as hard as you think it will be). How did you feel after you made the decision? Did you feel strong or weak? What happened?

Mentor's "Every-Meeting" Checklist

❑ Pray

❑ Encourage

❑ Share

❑ Challenge

Big Question #6: What Kind of People Does God Want in My Life?

Big Idea: We must select circles of people around us who help us grow and give us ministry opportunities, while making sure we don't let friends lead us into sin.

check in

1. How are you doing—*really?*
2. Did any interesting things come up in your journaling this week? Read or share a few thoughts from your journal.
3. How did the personal challenge from last week go? If you used it, ask, "Did you say no to anyone who asked you to do something you thought you shouldn't? How did that go?"

study (discussion questions)

1 Read Proverbs 27:17. How would you put into your own words what this means?

2 What's an example from your life of how this works?

3 Read 1 Thessalonians 5:11 and Hebrews 10:24–25. Why do you think God wants us to play this kind of role in each other's lives as Christians—why isn't the Bible alone sufficient motivation or encouragement?

4 Just as people can build us up, they can also tear us down. Read 1 Corinthians 15:33. Give an example of when you saw this happen in either your own life or that of someone you know.

5 Proverbs 16:28 and 22:24 – 25 note the characteristics of the kinds of people who can wound us. How do you think we can show love to people like this, while at the same time not letting them do us harm?

6 In extreme cases, we might need to separate ourselves from certain people until they are willing to change. In 1 Corinthians 5:9 – 11 and 2 Thessalonians 3:14 – 15, what does Paul say about the kind of person who presents the biggest threat to our spiritual well-being?

7 Jesus was called a "friend of sinners" (Matt. 11:19) and was scolded by religious leaders for hanging out with them at parties. Read Luke 5:29–32. What was Jesus' purpose in spending time with the "wrong" kind of people?

8 How can we do like Jesus, yet not be drawn into the wrong actions that others may engage in?

---

leader's note

One of the hardest things for students to do is to be among friends who are non-believers without becoming like them. Because as persons they are still "wet cement," students often bounce between extremes: they either go with the crowd and compromise their Christian witness, or they isolate themselves and become judgmental of their non-Christian acquaintances. Neither extreme serves the student or the kingdom, and you as their mentor can provide a great reality check to help them see when they go too far to one end of the continuum.

scripture memory

Do not be misled: "Bad company corrupts good character."

1 CORINTHIANS 15:33

how I see this verse applying to my life:

leader's note

Make sure the student has made the connection between this verse and "real life."

personal challenge

Suggestion for this week's challenge: Send a thank-you note or an email to the two people you identified as positive influences on your life.

my life

What two people would you like to thank for being a good influence on your life? (Think of at least one who is not a parent.) What are the qualities of the people that you value, and why do you consider those qualities so important? Who might include *your* name on such a list? How does that make you feel? Why? After you've written *about* those people who shaped you, why not write a note or an email *to* them?

Mentor's "Every-Meeting" Checklist

❑ Pray

❑ Encourage

❑ Share

❑ Challenge

a final word

Congratulations on completing your first six meetings and Be-With times with your student! By now you've got some confidence, and we hope you'll be able to keep going with even more enthusiasm. God is for you and is working in the student's life—and in yours—in ways you can see, and in many ways you can't see yet. Keep sowing, and in due time you'll harvest a rich reward (Galatians 6:9). And don't forget to look around you and recommend this book to someone else who could mentor a student. You—and they—are changing the world as you live out the Be-With Factor!

G-Force

Taking Your Relationship with God to a New Level

Bo Boshers

Ever feel tired of trying REALLY HARD to be a Christian?

Being a Christ-follower isn't about trying really hard; it's about training to be more like Jesus so he can transform you into the person he made you to be. *G-Force* shows you how.

The "Five Gs" of *G-Force* are markers or guides for your spiritual journey. They are designed to help take the guesswork out of what it really means to be a fully devoted follower of Christ—to live like Jesus would if he were in your place. In personal devotions and weekly small group gatherings, you'll learn about

Grace: Move beyond religious rules and regulations and learn how to live in God's grace—then learn how to share this grace with others.

Growth: Discover how spiritual practices can bring you closer to the heart of God.

Groups: Experience an authentic community where you will learn what it means to know and be known—to have real and intimate friendships throughout your life.

Gifts: Identify your spiritual gifts and dedicate them to serving God—then watch how God uses your gifts to impact the world in amazing ways.

Good Stewardship: Trust God with all your resources and discover what it means to live with freedom and generosity.

In each session you'll be challenged to think about what you really believe and learn how to have a deeper relationship with God and with others. Once you discover the power of G-Force, you learn that being a Christian is ultimately about Christ with you and within you, guiding and empowering you to become more like him.

Softcover: 0-310-24446-3

Pick up a copy today at your favorite bookstore!

Student Ministry for the 21st Century

Transforming Your Youth Group into a Vital Student Ministry

Bo Boshers with Kim Anderson

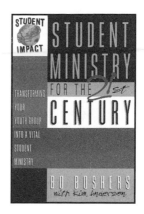

Why settle for a "youth group" when you can build a dynamic student ministry that keeps more and more students coming—and keeps them growing!

From the director of Student Impact, one of the country's largest and most effective student ministries, here is a clear, step-by-step approach that takes you for a quantum leap beyond merely

Maintaining a Youth Group ...	to Building a Student Ministry
Activity-driven	Purpose-driven
Unclear vision	Clear vision
Inward focus, content with the "clique"	Outward focus, compassion for lost people
Minimum growth	Consistent growth
Songs and games	Worship and prayer
Keeps the traditions	Evaluates for effectiveness
"Babysitting"	Impacting the world

Softcover: 0-310-20122-5

Pick up a copy today at your favorite bookstore!

ZONDERVAN™

GRAND RAPIDS, MICHIGAN 49530 USA

WWW.ZONDERVAN.COM

WILLOW

Willow Creek Resources

Willow Creek Association
Vision, Training, Resources for Prevailing Churches

This resource was created to serve you and to help you build a local church that prevails. It is just one of many ministry tools that are part of the Willow Creek Resources® line, published by the Willow Creek Association together with Zondervan.

The Willow Creek Association (WCA) was created in 1992 to serve a rapidly growing number of churches from across the denominational spectrum that are committed to helping unchurched people become fully devoted followers of Christ. Membership in the WCA now numbers over 10,500 Member Churches worldwide from more than ninety denominations.

The Willow Creek Association links like-minded Christian leaders with each other and with strategic vision, training, and resources in order to help them build prevailing churches designed to reach their redemptive potential. Here are some of the ways the WCA does that.

- **A2: Building Prevailing Acts 2 Churches—Today**—an annual two-and-a-half day event, held at Willow Creek Community Church in South Barrington, Illinois, to explore strategies for building churches that reach out to seekers and build believers, and to discover new innovations and breakthroughs from Acts 2 churches around the country.

- **The Leadership Summit**—a once a year, two-and-a-half-day conference to envision and equip Christians with leadership gifts and responsibilities. Presented live at Willow Creek as well as via satellite broadcast to over one hundred locations across North

America, this event is designed to increase the leadership effectiveness of pastors, ministry staff, volunteer church leaders, and Christians in the marketplace.

- **Ministry-Specific Conferences**—throughout each year the WCA hosts a variety of conferences and training events—both at Willow Creek's main campus and offsite, across the U.S., and around the world—targeting church leaders and volunteers in ministry-specific areas such as: evangelism, small groups, preaching and teaching, the arts, children, students, women, volunteers, stewardship, raising up resources, etc.

- **Willow Creek Resources®**—provides churches with trusted and field-tested ministry resources in such areas as leadership, evangelism, spiritual formation, spiritual gifts, small groups, stewardship, student ministry, children's ministry, the use of the arts-drama, media, contemporary music—and more.

- **WCA Member Benefits**—includes substantial discounts to WCA training events, a 20 percent discount on all Willow Creek Resources®, *Defining Moments* monthly audio journal for leaders, quarterly *Willow* magazine, access to a Members-Only section on WillowNet, monthly communications, and more. Member Churches also receive special discounts and premier services through WCA's growing number of ministry partners—Select Service Providers—and save an average of $500 annually depending on the level of engagement.

For specific information about WCA conferences, resources, membership, and other ministry services contact:

Willow Creek Association
P.O. Box 3188
Barrington, IL 60011-3188
Phone: 847-570-9812
Fax: 847-765-5046
www.willowcreek.com

We want to hear from you. Please send your comments about this
book to us in care of zreview@zondervan.com. Thank you.

GRAND RAPIDS, MICHIGAN 49530 USA

ZONDERVAN.COM/
AUTHOR**TRACKER**